It is nigh on forty years since I arrived at Kensal Green – a young vagabond fresh out of Drama School and clutching a pristine Equity Card – I was there to join Theatre Centre.

Groups of 4 or 6 actors (one of whom would be Company Manager and driver) took off across the country in vans with props, costumes, rostra, make-up, ironing boards: all the paraphernalia of performance. We earned £7 a week and still managed to find digs and have a slap up three course dinner once a week!

And we learned: to be diplomats, facilitators; how to control and recapture the attention and imaginations of our young audiences with nuances of performance, changes of pitch, face, inflection and movement. You could say we almost knew what it was like to be a club comic on a wet night in Burnley! One time I had 'the law' knocking on my door. The van was parked in the street. Somebody had looked through the rear window and seen a bowl with blood in it: MURDER! In those days a policeman would believe you when you said you were a member of a theatre group performing a piece that included an Inca sacrifice.

Thank you Theatre Centre and Brian Way for giving me such valuable experience at the start of my acting career and for enriching the experience and exercising the imagination muscle of many youngsters from Infant School to Youth Club age.

Happy Birthday!

Pam St. Clement

Small Business Computing

-Keeping it Simple-

What we do?

- Free consultancy and general advice
- Flexible support packages and preventative maintenance
- Bespoke servers, network design and installation
- Internet service, ADSL & leased lines
- Communication & security solutions
- Hardware & software sales
- System and user training
- Database design
- Disaster recovery

Why choose us?

- Friendly and experienced technical team
- Technical support 8am – 8pm (24/7 option available)
- Free support period on all installations
- Specialists in infrastructure for charities and schools

Special Discounts
for
Schools
Colleges
& Charities

Please call us now for an informal chat!

Small Business Computin
Phone: 0800 298 6830
Fax: 020 7691 7140
www.smallbizcomputing.com
enquiries@smallbizcomputing.com

Theatre Centre
plays for young people

introduced by
Rosamunde Hutt

Listen To Your Parents
Benjamin Zephaniah

Precious
Angela Turvey

Look At Me
Anna Reynolds

Gorgeous
Anna Furse

Glow
Manjinder Virk

Souls
Roy Williams

AURORA METRO PRESS

Contents

*Theatre Centre would like to thank
everyone involved in the development of
these six plays and their productions.
There are many unsung heroes and heroines
who make Theatre Centre's work possible,
especially the teachers who book our shows
and young people whose honest responses
frustrate, challenge, delight and inspire us
to write on...*

Introduction

The gift

In 1953 Dorothy L. Sayers gave the first £250 to help start Theatre Centre. I relish the fact that it was a dramatist, a great twentieth century crime writer and a classical scholar, who made such a practical contribution to the creation of art. Sayers was taking the long view, thinking ahead, taking the leap of faith, investing in the future.

Fifty years on there is much to celebrate. This anthology is just a glimpse of the company's extensive body of work. In this introduction I would like to share with you our playwriting processes. These start with the first conversations about theme and content and end, not in the bar on the opening night, but only when the set is finally stored away after a three month tour and the production photographs are placed in the Theatre Centre archives, cheek by jowl with those from the hundreds of new plays that the company has produced.

Commissioning: how, why and who

When commissioning we look for ideas that touch a chord, asking ourselves: is this contemporary? Is this relevant? And always, does this put something new in the school hall?

Crucially, we also take our inspiration to commission from an image that sings or shouts at us – with *Gorgeous* it was Anna Furse's concept of a shape-shifter, a girl who at times is as thin as a reed, living on celery and water, and then becomes gigantic, devouring whole grocery stores to satisfy her hunger.

For some projects we start with the writer. I asked Roy Williams, 'What do you want to write? Who do you want to write for?' *Souls* was already inside Roy waiting to get out. We offered him the space to create. Angela Turvey knew the territory that she wanted to explore. She said to me, 'It's about a girl called Precious' – we started from there.

Or sometimes it is the theme. Mercury Theatre's Associate Director, Adrian Stokes, was keen to look at the lives and experiences of young people who are at risk and patterns and cycles of violence or bad behaviour. *Look at Me* by Anna Reynolds was the result.

Sometimes we move forward from a hunch, an instinct, a belief that this writer has the capacity to speak to the audience. On a writers' residency we arranged, Manjinder Virk's first few scenes from *Glow* flew off the page – we were sure her work would develop into a brave and beautiful play.

Exceptionally, it is the play – Benjamin Zephaniah's *Listen To Your Parents* was a must – we broke one cardinal rule ('we don't do existing plays at Theatre Centre') to ensure that this piece reached school audiences.

We discover our writers through networking – sometimes they find us, and sometimes we find them. We see shows, we start a dialogue, and we create new relationships through workshops that match writers with mentors. It is important to us that the writers care about our audiences and it is central to our ethos that we enable our writers to write from the heart, not fitting into a preconceived set of givens. We are always interested in the gaps, giving chances to those who are under-represented in the theatre industry. We commit ourselves to writers, very few write just one piece for us. leading playwrights who have helped make Theatre Centre what it is today (please see the list at the end of this book) regularly return to us later in their careers, creating sophisticated theatre for young audiences, born out of their years of experience.

Development and Dramaturgy

Following the commitment – you're on. We'll get the contract to you next week, the show will tour in the autumn in two years' time – we move forward in partnership: pupils, teachers, artists, administrators; listening to gut instincts about what is working and what is not, as we read the emerging script. There is rigorous development through in-house 'try outs' (rehearsed readings) and nuts and bolts dramaturgy. Guest dramaturges and guest directors play as strong a part as I do, as Theatre Centre's Director. We state that we are writer-led but paradoxically (and hopefully harmoniously) there are moments of intervention. 'Do you really need that character?' 'Imagine if... ' 'Let's pretend... 'At all times we try to tease out the best process for the individual writer. Some need to be left alone, some value long talks at key moments, others benefit from walks around the block. A lot of tea is drunk.

We also test the material with our target audience. These plays have all been written against a background of creative writing with young people. At times, writers discover new corners of their text through direct engagement with their audiences. We get a first draft or a few scenes which we take into a school; we hear young people's voices, their responses. We reflect – the writer uses what is valuable, what enhances the piece – we return with the show and gain feedback. For some writers it is invaluable, for others it may only subtly shift the kaleidoscope. The process is collaborative but the plays are never written by committee. Our goal is two-fold: to do all that we can to release what the writer wants to say, and to try to break down the barriers between those who make and those who receive the work.

Plays can take from one to three years to evolve. Writers endorse our in-depth approach. New writers are trained in a rigorous and challenging 'school', mature writers can flex their wings and take risks.

Language: of text, aesthetic, theatre

For us, 'The Play's The Thing'. Detailed attention to character, form, structure, plot and theme allows the plays to be adventurous and imaginative theatrically. We relish the presence of the actor, ensuring communication and connection. The play is the catalyst – everything flows from it – its worlds, its themes and its process. Our plays are often controversial, always on the pulse. We look for intriguing combinations of cultural references, in word and image. We travel nationwide. It is a necessity for us to reflect our audiences' lives and experiences. Jamaican *patois*, Asian dialect, British street language, the mother tongue – all find their place. The character of Alice in *Gorgeous* was played by a British-Iranian actress, Viss Elliot.

In our production Alice's mother spoke in Iranian at the climax of the piece and Graeme Miller's score drew on Iranian music.

One of our central objectives is developing artistic language for our audiences and thereby developing theatre writing. Many of our writers wish to experiment with form and structure, juxtaposing different time scales, exploding the conventional narrative and fracturing time. *Look at Me* plays with past and present. Direct address is often used, creating dynamic relationships between actor and spectator.

One of the countless attractions of Benjamin Zephaniah's *Listen To Your Parents* was, of course, the chance to present his poetry to our audiences. We called it a theatre poem, moved by the rhythms that were present in both the preaching and the beating.

The journey through the 1990's into the 21st Century

Over the past decade we have identified three major cycles in our work: *Rites of Passage, Examining Contemporary Culture* and *Releasing the Authentic Voice*, following on Theatre Centre's groundbreaking tradition of telling hidden histories or unlocking silenced voices. Fifty per cent of our output is now written by black and Asian writers, affirming our track record as a uniquely diverse commissioning company. We have encouraged writers to begin with childhood – children's memories, emotions of childhood, lost childhoods, shattered childhoods, the joyfulness of children, affirmation of play. Writers have explored the territory of roots, belonging, home, exile, otherness and difference. Over the years we have seen the points of interest shift. Whereas Angela Turvey's first play for us in 1995, *A Fine Example*, looked at life here and in Jamaica, in *Precious* (2003), Jamaica is no longer so present, though it still casts its spell. We have moved into the world of the explorer, the adventurer, the artist. Creativity has remained a strong *leitmotif*; central characters who want to write (Benjamin's footballer-poet, Mark) or paint (Angela's artist, Precious). Coping with life's big transitions is a key element in our work – dealing with change (the adolescents in *Look at Me* and *Gorgeous*) and coming to terms with death (the brothers in *Souls*, Kul and Raj in *Glow*).

Building the body of work

Theatre Centre plays are commissioned separately, although all fit into a landscape of ideas and themes. We hope that our work opens doors to the imagination, to understanding, to glimpses of possible utopias, to creativity. I have always seen myself akin to a curator, choosing each work for itself, its passion and potential. But as in an art gallery, once you see all the pieces displayed, you start to see the connections and the common threads. Much of our current body of work looks at the outsider, the family, violence, masculinity, being a young woman in the modern world, the relationship between Britain, India and the Caribbean, the pressures on the adult, the parent, the young person and the longing to make your mark.

We are working to an agenda that is consistently about making the brave choices, embracing danger and complexity, presenting the unexpected. Two men embrace and one weeps in *Souls*. Pupils write to us about how they appreciate seeing men trying and failing and trying again to communicate. We are making theatre that makes a difference, illuminating complex and emotional issues, accessing and witnessing real life situations through the safe distance of fictionalised characters and events.

The future

Crucially we commission to produce. We occasionally have worked in laboratory style, testing out ideas that don't see the light of day. But usually once the leap of faith is made, the plays get done. They are performed in the harsh light of the school hall under a real audience's gaze, (a sleepy teenager at ten a.m., vocal critics on a Friday afternoon) with the watchful eye of time seeing whether they will stand its test. We believe in a huge investment in these pieces of work and try to offer a longer life. *Souls* has toured three times, including to the first European Urban Theatre Festival in Holland, which examined cultural identity in our modern world. *Look at Me* toured twice and *Gorgeous* has been seen, at the invitation of the British Council, in the Philippines and Malaysia where the Victorian girl's corset was compared to the foot-breaking required to fit tiny Chinese shoes.

The great problem with new writing is that the play is done and then disappears. Very few new plays for young people get published. Wherever I go, people often say to me, 'Can I buy the script?' At least now I can offer something tangible. I hope that people will handle this book, scribble in the margins, underline key passages, improvise around the themes, write poetry inspired by the writing... This anthology presents only six plays specifically for teenagers and young adults from the last decade. Our goal is to publish all our plays.

In this, our Golden Anniversary Year, we are looking for new voices, new visions, the next generation of artists and audiences. Of the writers represented here Manjinder Virk and Angela Turvey received their first full commissions from Theatre Centre. Looking back at the archives, this can be said of many playwrights, now highly regarded, award-winning, mentors to fledgling playwrights.

This Autumn we are marking the career of Charles Way, who started to write at Theatre Centre as a young writer-in-residence in 1979, with a new production of *A Spell Of Cold Weather,* as well as showcasing the work of young writers still at school, in *Reality Check,* part of our Authentic Voices programme. Back in 1953 Dorothy L. Sayers was investing in the future: so must we. We need to sustain and celebrate our playwrights – those that give us new ways of looking at the world.

Rosamunde Hutt
Director, Theatre Centre

On the road with Theatre Centre

8.30am at a primary school somewhere in England. Theatre Centre's van moves cautiously into the car park. Inside the school, two members of the touring company are introducing themselves to the school secretary. She is unaware that a theatre group was expected. The teacher who made the booking is not in school today – she has had to attend a training seminar, elsewhere. There doesn't seem to be any record... The Head pops into the office. She recalls something – she was asked whether the parents would object to something in a play – seemed fine, but can't remember any more. Anyway, there are millions of things to do, so she can't really help, but good luck!

The rest of the company materialise and the Company Stage Manager takes charge. The Confirmation Form shows the details of the booking – 'Can we just get on and prepare?' 'Yes, fine but you do know that there's assembly today?' 'No!' 'Yes, it's usually tomorrow but because of a trip it has been moved to today. The hall will be free at 9.30. You could put your things in the hall then and if you could do your performance at 9.45 because...'

Other members of the company, wisely keeping out of the way during the negotiations, remember different times. The world of the rehearsal room, the work with the director and movement director seem far away. The fulfilment of those weeks – working with a writer to mould a script into performance readiness, learning the songs with the composer, seeing the set grow and costumes appear – seems to be fading in the lobby of this school. Thoughts turn to the set: to be unloaded, set up and then put back in the van afterwards. A daily ordeal! And last night's B&B had barely provided bed or breakfast. Tired, disheartened, morale dipping...

At the opposite end of the country, another team of performers are in the gym at a secondary school. Until the new drama studio is built, this sweaty arena is where the theatre must breathe. Although the van had to be driven across a field, the get-in was easy, with school caretakers and some drama students helping; a warm welcome. The teacher books Theatre Centre's shows repeatedly. GCSE, B-Tec and A-level students can use the play and the performance for their coursework. The text is available, the education resources are comprehensive and now include a specially made video with rehearsal scenes, interviews with the cast and creative teams, and background information. Perhaps the students at this particular school helped Theatre Centre develop the play, months before the finished production reaches them. If so, they are keen to see which of their ideas and thoughts find their way into what they are about to see. Even with a bright, enthusiastic audience and a wonderful hosting drama teacher, distractions still occur. Bells ring – and always at crucial, quiet moments! Dinner ladies chat behind serving hatch shutters. A lost class wanders in. Some teachers still use the short cut between sites which lies through the back of the space. Doors clatter, keys rattle, shoes squeak. The acoustics of the space resemble those of a major cathedral, yet, if you turn just a bit that way, a shout is a whisper. Inevitably, the reluctants have commandeered seats in the back rows and keep up their own commentary, some of which even concerns the play. This is the crucible of acting talent, the place where only the best survive. If they can do this, they really can do anything.

After the performance, the drama teacher is pleased, most students have responded positively. It was less expensive and – just about – less hassle than going on a trip. But there are questions and criticisms: why is Theatre Centre commissioning this kind of work? Why is the play so male / female / conventional / baffling / real / unreal... The young people would prefer... they need to see... we're tired of... It is all noted, it all goes into the company's thinking, it all guides the choices that are made about writers, directors, styles.

One of the many appealing factors of schools touring is that the contact with the audience is so immediate. Responses can't be disguised; feedback, once provoked, is torrential. Tomorrow, the cast is to begin a run in a lovely studio theatre. The lighting design will be used again, and it will be great to have proper dressing rooms. School and college parties will mingle with 'ordinary' audience members; if all has been well prepared – and utlising this kind of work depends on thorough preparation – the event will be vibrant, giving hope for a healthy future of theatre-going. Creating this intimacy, this naked relationship with an audience which can be found in schools, will be the aim in every space the company visits.

Two hundred and fifty miles away, another performance has just ended. Through forbearance, compromise, good humour and dedication the team have got the show on. It looks as if it has been worthwhile. There is a buzz in the hall. Despite the best efforts of the CSM, the children are keen to invade the set to meet their favourite characters. The boy who had to go out because the play was upsetting him – for reasons to do with his family, the teacher later explains – is at least copying a bit of the action with his friend. Others are singing one of the songs, which, through constant repetition in the weeks ahead, will drive parents and teachers mad and prove the biggest threat to Theatre Centre getting a return booking. There is a sense of amazement at the *scale* of what has been presented in 'our hall'. The depth of the story, the quality of the acting, the beauty of the set and of the music, the movement, the sound effects, the costumes. At this moment a new audience for theatre has been won, a new generation inspired. What happens next is still far from certain.

The Plays

Listen To Your Parents by Benjamin Zephaniah – set against the backdrop of domestic violence, this portrayal of teenage life and ambition is deeply moving. Zephaniah's poetry imbues the piece with rhythm and flavour. Religion, patriarchy and the sense of being a refugee, even at home, are the unsettling themes running through the play.

Precious by Angela Turvey – decisions made at a young age are filtered through bitter adult experience in a tender, beautifully-written piece centred in the experience of black and Asian women as generations clash and art and life combine.

Look At Me by Anna Reynolds – a highly sophisticated stage technique allows Reynolds to tell the stories of two young women facing exclusion from mainstream education. Gritty, hard, witty and fast paced, the play will test actors and directors of every generation.

Gorgeous by Anna Furse – a Victorian girl, Alice, moves through time and body shapes in an unflinching portrait of self-image and eating disorders in young women. In the original production this was a one-woman show but the inventive script gives many opportunities for different production styles.

Glow by Manjinder Virk – a pulsating, extrovert debut play about the will to fight for what you want, the desire to have some magic in life and fraught relationships with role models. Uncompromising in asking today's second and third generation Britons: 'Who are you?' – Virk's writing stings like bee!

Souls by Roy Williams – three brothers from a black British family struggle to connect with each other emotionally in the wake of their mother's death and under the shadow of their father's suicide. Written in vibrant dialogue, the play unlocks the problems men have with communicating their feelings, with making choices and facing up to responsibilities.

Listen to your Parents Julie Hewlett and Kevin G. Neil (Photo: Robert Day)

Precious Natasha Narcisse and Mina Barber (Photo: Hugo Glendinning)

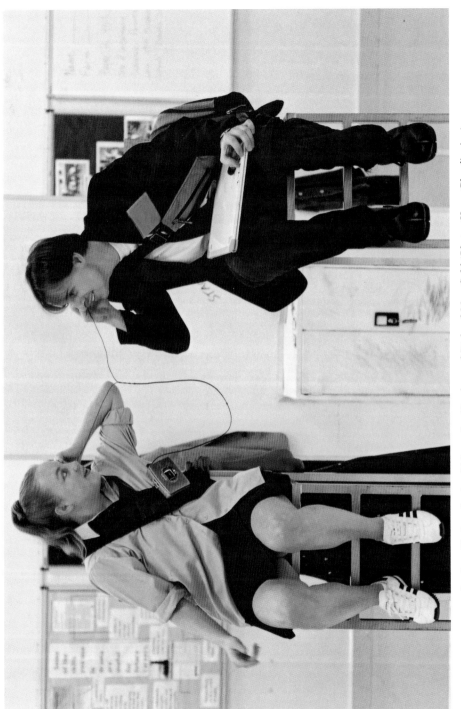

Look at Me (production 2) Lorraine Stanley and Richard Mansfield (Photo: Hugo Glendinning)

Gorgeous Viss Elliot (Photo: Timothy Nunn)

Glow Nina Bhirangi and Anthony Mark Barrow (Photo: Robert Day)

Souls (tour 2) Wole Sawyerr and Michael Conrad [Alex - Lincoln James] (Photo: Hugo Glendinning)

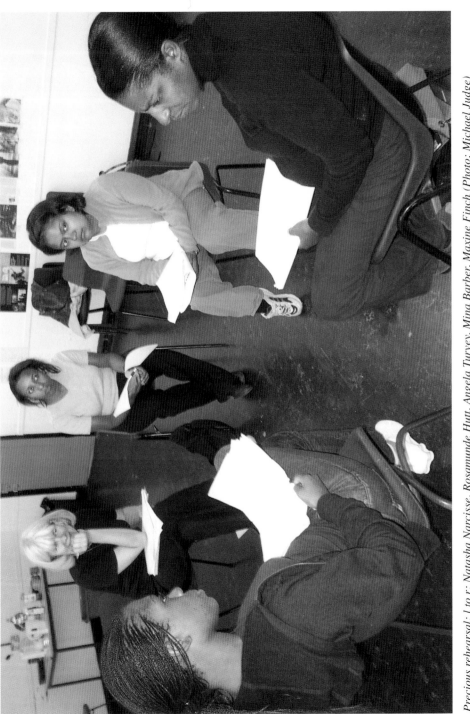

Precious rehearsal; 1 to r: Natasha Narcisse, Rosamunde Hutt, Angela Turvey, Mina Barber, Maxine Finch (Photo: Michael Judge)

Authentic Voices / Reality Check workshop led by Co-director Noël Greig with Nasima Begum and Fahima Nessa (Photo: Michael Judge)

Listen To Your Parents

Listen To Your Parents

As I listened to the Afternoon Play on Radio 4 in the Spring of 2001, I became increasingly drawn into a world which was both fascinating and deeply shocking. *Listen To Your Parents* is a heart-rending tale of ambition, hope, desperation, poverty and violence. It was told in the language of poetic fantasy, with wry and ironic humour in a vocabulary which spoke across the generations and cultural divides. Its final lines were some of the most shocking and profoundly moving words that I have heard spoken by a character on radio.

Some weeks later, after a theatre award ceremony I cornered Rosamunde Hutt and thrust the radio script into her hand, telling her that I thought this would make a wonderful play for young people. Both Theatre Centre and Nottingham Playhouse Roundabout have a long tradition of making new work for audiences of young people, usually in non-theatre settings. Both companies develop relationships with writers and implicit in the working processes are periods of development when those artists are given the freedom to experiment without the pressures of an audience. So a working draft of a theatre version was created by Benjamin which we took to schools in North London. There we observed the responses of our audience members as we tried out a variety of scenes, discussed their reactions to the material and gathered a body of information that would guide us towards our final product.

It was the challenges of the script that ultimately made it so worthwhile. The central character was younger than the target audience, the geography of the piece was foreign in almost every sense, the physicality of the playing was, and had to be, deeply shocking whilst the final revelation provoked gasps in every performance I attended during its three month run.

It asks serious questions about our society and the ways in which we treat fellow humans, it proffers alternatives and ultimately hope for the future through the debates which the text in performance inspires. It is therefore part of a serious tradition of provoking its audiences to look long and hard at our society and do something about its improvement.

Andrew Breakwell
Director of Roundabout & Education, Nottingham Playhouse

Listen To Your Parents

Benjamin Zephaniah

*Winner of the Commission for Racial Equality
Race in the Media Award, 2001.*

Produced in collaboration with Nottingham Playhouse Roundabout
TIE. First performance was on 10th September 2002, Nottingham.
Directed by Paul J. Medford, designed by Jane Linz Roberts.
Lighting designed by Nick Richings

MARK	**Mark Nicolson**
WALI	**Richard Sumitro**
MOM	**Julie Hewlett**
DAD	**Kevin G. Neil**
VOICES	church congregation and crowd of kids.

Company Stage Managers – Patrick Nelson / Dan Hyman
Fight direction – Nicholas Hall
Accent advice – Jan Haydn Rowles
Voice Consultant/Casting – Bernadette O'Brien (Associate Artist)
Dramaturgical support – Esther Richardson
Education Resources – Michael Judge & Allie Spencer
Graphic Design – Bahnhof
Production Photography – Robert Day
For Nottingham Playhouse:
Andrew Breakwell – Director of Roundabout and Education
Kitty Parker – Roundabout Administrator
Production Manager – Nicky Hudswell
Casting – Sooki McShane
Originally commissioned and broadcast by BBC Radio 4 in 2000.
With thanks to: Damian Asher, Clinton Blake, Michael Conrad, Charlie
Folorunsho, Sami Hargreaves, Arnie Hewitt and Irma Inniss for script
development; Angela Turvey (Theatre Centre /London Arts Board Diverse
Acts writer in residence 2001/2002); teachers and students at Bethnal Green
Technology College, Mount Carmel School (London) and Coopers'
Company and Coburn School (Upminster).

Note:
The play is set in and around the home of the Campbells, a Black British family living in Birmingham. The Campbell family consists of Mark and his Mom and Dad – his sister Angela and baby Carlton need not appear.

1. MONDAY

Mark is sitting on his bed looking in his bag.
Wali addresses the audience from a platform/pulpit.

WALI   On the first day God created the heavens and the Earth. Then he created flowers and trees, and humans beings and living stuff that creep upon the surface of the Earth. And he looked down upon the Earth and he saw that it was good. Then for some strange reason he created school. And mark Campbell attended one such school in the great land known as Birmingham. And it was there that Mark Campbell created a great opportunity for himself, and he went for it.

They both break into football terrace style chants.

BOTH   Villa *(clap, clap, clap)* Villa *(clap, clap, clap)* Villa *(clap, clap, clap)*

Mark addresses the audience.

MARK   Yes this is it, I can't wait. I could be playing for Aston Villa. Me, Aston Villa, brilliant innit? And here it is, look at this, *(Takes shirt out of bag)* – me Aston Villa shirt. I wanted the whole kit but Mom said she couldn't afford it, but the shirt's OK, no it's more than OK, it's wicked guy. I wasn't even doing any-thing special, just playing around on the pitch after school and I could see this bloke standing there with Mr. Collins the P.E. teacher. At first I thought he was a parent or something. Then when we finished playing Mr Collins called me over and I thought, O, O, I'm in trouble again, but I wasn't. The bloke said, 'I've heard a lot about you Mark. What are you doing next

Saturday afternoon?' So I said, 'Playing football,' and he said, 'Do you want to go to Villa Park and play some football?' And I said, 'What actually *in* Villa Park?' And he said, 'Yes lad, we're having trials, we're looking for some players for the junior team and you look pretty good to me. And then I started to tell him that I wasn't even playing me best today and that I usually score about three goals in every game, and that I play even better on a full-size pitch, but he said I should save all me energy for Saturday. *(Mark chants)* Villa, Villa, Villa.

Music.
Mark picks up his book and begins to read.

MARK

Red ripe Mangoes on Lozzell's Road,
Ackees on Heatfield,
And Callaloo for all on Witton Road,
Jamaica must be here somewhere.

There's Reggae in the morning
Reggae at noon
And Reggae is played on Soho Road at night
For grown ups and foxes alike.
Jamaica must be here somewhere.

Coconuts and cashew nuts cook themselves,
And the aunties and the uncles
Walk like they have springs in their feet
And drums on their minds,
Is this Jamaica?

Jamaica must be here somewhere,
I can taste it,
I can smell it,
Everybody is talking about it,
There are Jamaican newspapers in the corner shops
And Jamaican curls in my hair,

You can't fool me.
Jamaica must be here somewhere.
(Pause)
I got two of these books, both exactly the same, one for me and
one for me Mom. I wrote the poems meself and sellotaped them
together. Look, see what it says there? Published by Mark
Anthony Campbell – Limited. And there's the title, it's called
'Life'.

Lights fade.

2.

*In the next room, Mother and Father are in bed when the baby starts
crying. Mom goes to comfort baby.*

MOM   OK lovely, what's the matter? What is it, your belly?
You got wind? Now don't tell me you want milk cause you just
had your milk – so what's the matter with my little darling?
(Baby cries even louder) Come, come now, what's the matter
beautiful? What can I do for you pretty boy, hey?

DAD   I wish that baby would shut up. How the hell am I
suppose to work if I can't get a good night sleep? I get it in me
ear hole every night from that child. How the hell am I suppose to
earn money if I can't get a decent night sleep?

MOM   What do you want me to do? I mean what do you
expect, it's a baby you know, babies cry, that's what they do.
Gosh what's wrong with you, you used to complain when Mark
used to cry. You used to complain when Angela used to cry, now
you've started complaining again, but hey, you never complained
when it came to making babies. Oh no, you didn't have any
complaints then. In fact you were very keen, too keen if you ask
me.

DAD   Shut up woman.

MOM   Now look at you, you want me to shut up, you want
baby to shut up, you want Angela to shut up, and you want Mark
to shut up. But why don't you shut up, do you know how to shut
up? Because from what I've heard you was the biggest cry-baby

in Edgbaston, and from where I'm sitting it looks as if you haven't stop crying yet.

Mark addresses the audience as if to distract their attention from his parents' argument.

MARK   Wali Ahmad, he comes to my school, he's me best friend, he thinks I'm a bit weird. He said that I should mek up me mind about what I want to be, a poet or a footballer. I told him I wanna be both, Eric Cantona did, he was a poet and a footballer and his poetry didn't stop him from being a good player, did it? But sometimes I think the rest of his team didn't understand him, they thought he was a bit soft.

Sound of baby crying gets louder.

DAD   Shut up, child.

MOM   You shouting at him ain't gonna help, is it? Maybe if you tried picking him up and showing him a bit of love, maybe that would help.

DAD   Who me?

MOM   Yes you, who else?

DAD   Stop being lippy and get that baby to shut the hell up, I wanna get some –

MOM *(interrupting)* What do you mean get that baby to shut the hell up? It's a baby just in case you haven't noticed, a living breathing thing, do you think I can get him to stop crying just like that, well if you really think that's the way it is, *you* get him to stop crying.

DAD   Getting him to stop crying is not my job woman, it's your job, that ain't a man thing, it's a woman thing, that's your business, now sort it out.

Light on Mark.

MARK *(to audience)* I've lived here all me life, born in Aston, well Dudley Road hospital nearby. Supported Villa all me life. So next

Saturday I'm gonna wear me Villa shirt with pride. Yes guy, I'm gonna big it up, I mean, I don't know any Aston Villa player that's a poet and I don't know any Aston Villa player that's born in Aston, so I'm gonna be different, trust me, the original you know what I mean? True Villa fan, true Villa style.

DAD   You just be careful how you answer me back, you know what I'm saying woman. Don't get me angry now, all I want is a good night sleep, some peace and quiet and a good night's sleep, and if you was a decent mother you would know how to keep your children quiet, and you wouldn't be speaking to me like that.

MOM   And if you was a decent father you would have some more patience with you children, and you would have some respect for your wife, you can't go on like this you know, you go on all religious so don't you know that judgement will come, don't you know that God will find you? You say you're a man, so live like a man.

DAD   Yes and you're a woman so just shut your big mouth and stop answering me back. Remember this, I run tings, right? I control the scene, you must know that no woman will never rule me, I have dominion, and is god give me that, so just rest it.

Light on Mark.

MARK   When I came home from school and told me Mom that I was going for trials she was happy guy, she's cool, but I ain't even told me Dad yet. He didn't give me a chance to say any-thing – when he came home from work the first thing he did was send me and Angela to bed and start shouting at me Mom and that's all he's been doing all night, shouting. *(sarcastically)* Angela's all asleep, in her little bed, with her little dolls, and her little plaits on her little head. Boy can she sleep. Sometimes she can't even get up in the morning. When she grows up and she's my age she could go for trials because they have girls' teams now, you know, and if I teach her everything I know she'll be

good, won't she? I wanna sleep now. It ain't Carlton's fault, is it?
He's just a baby.

Click. Lights fade.

MARK   Good night.

2. TUESDAY
Wali addresses the audience from platform/pulpit.

WALI   On the second day, Mark did forty press-ups, 'cause
press-ups help build upper body strength, and upper body strength
is needed if you want to be a powerful winger. And on that day,
in the land of the Brummie, Mark also done forty squats, twenty
jumping jacks, and his knees were brought unto his chest two
score and six times, and that was before his cornflakes,
not bad hey.

Mark is playing invisible football in his room.

MARK   Four more days and I'll be there, Villa Park.
And it's Mark Campbell doing a thing,
Yes, it's Mark Campbell on the right wing,
Look at Mark Campbell, he's on a roll,
Here comes Mark Campbell... yes, it's a goal. *(Pause)*
Hey, you know something, one thing I haven't done yet is write a
football poem, well come to think about it, I just did. Sometimes
poems just come like that. You can't force poems, you can't just
say OK today I will be inspired, inspiration can come at any time.
No one knows where inspiration comes from, if I knew where
inspiration came from I'd go there wouldn't I? It can come when
you're working, or when you're eating, or it could come like it
says in the Bible, 'Like a thief in the night.' Well, it doesn't say
inspiration will come like a thief in the night, it says *the day of
the Lord* will. Before I decided that I wanted to be a poet, I
thought I wanted to be like me Dad, a preacher in a church like,
but then I changed me mind.

4.

In Church. Dad is at the pulpit preaching loudly.

DAD   And when we look in the world we see wars and rumours of war, we see spiritual wickedness in high and low places, oh my God. We see a world where people do not know their left from their right and their right from their left because they have been tricked by the ways of the world. Let me hear you say, 'Amen.'

CROWD   Amen.

DAD   Let me hear you say, Hallelujah.

CROWD   Hallelujah.

DAD   This is a dirty world.

MEMBERS OF THE CROWD Yes, yes.

DAD   This is a wicked world.

MEMBERS OF THE CROWD Tell them brother. Truth.

DAD   This is a world where children are having children, this is a world full of greed and envy. This is a world where children have no respect for their elders and this is a world where elders have no respect for God. This is Sodom and Gomorrah.

Big crowd response.

DAD   And if we not careful, people, we shall be like Lot's wife, who turn into a pillar of salt, why? Because she looked back. That's why when we leave this world we must not look back, praise God.

CROWD   Praise God. Hallelujah.

DAD   We must not be like the weak woman, unclean and unholy, and we must resist the temptations on the flesh.

Light on Mark.

MARK *(to audience)* I listen to me Dad and Pastor Bailey and some of the other people preaching in the church, and they're shouting loud and sweating, and banging the tables and stamping their feet and waving the Bible around, and I thought, God man, did Jesus preach like this? I don't think so.

DAD *(still preaching)* But what is going wrong? We need to analyse the situation and consider what is to be done. We need to ask ourselves, what it is that we need to do, to save ourselves from the brimstone and the fire. Well, my people, the answer is simple, praise the Lord. The truth is that this is not a complex or a difficult thing. We must do two things, Hallelujah. We must let the world know that Christ is not history, Christ is living, Christ is now, and we must put back the Lord Jesus Christ into our lives, we must bring Jesus right into the culture of society. Christ must be the inspiration for all of our politicians, Christ must be the inspiration for all of our teachers, he will lead us out of the darkness, he will lead us into the light, Christ himself must lead the way. Thank God.

Crowd response.

DAD　　　　　Praise Jesus. And secondly, we must rebuild the family – the family is the rock that holds up society. If you don't have discipline in the family, how can we have discipline in the schools? If you don't have discipline in the family, how can we have discipline in the factories? How in the name of God, can we have discipline on the streets, if there is no discipline in the family? God is the father, God is the son, God created families for us because families work best. Let me hear you praise the Lord.

CROWD　　　　Praise the Lord.
DAD　　　　　Let me hear you say, Hallelujah.
CROWD　　　　Hallelujah!

Light on Mark.

MARK *(turning to audience)* I reckon Jesus spoke soft and quietly like. I reckon he had manners, you know what I mean? He would say great wise things that would make people be 'Cool', bet he would drop phat lyrics guy, I don't think he'd be shouting his mouth off like a mad man.

DAD   We have moved so far away from the word of the Lord, that there are families today where the woman thinks that she is the head of the house, and that she has rights over the man. Some women today will actually say, that they want to be independent and they want to be in control. So this is suppose to be liberation, this is suppose to be progress, this is suppose to be the modern world, them call it feminism, *(laughs sarcastically)* but I know... and God knows... this is wrongism. *(Crowd laughs)* This is Satanism. Don't take my word for it; let us go to the Bible for guidance. It is written in the Book of Ephesians Chapter Five. 'Submitting yourselves one to another in the fear of God. Wives, submit yourselves unto your own husband as unto the Lord. For the husband is the head of the wife, even as Christ is the head of the church. Amen. *(Pause)*
These words are not made up by me, people. *(Pause)*
But I am saying to you today, we must work towards rebuilding back the family. Men know yourselves, and know your responsibilities, and woman, know that God has said man is the head, so submit yourselves to him, and praise the Lord.

Crowd goes wild.

5.

MARK *(to audience)* The preachers say they want to be like Jesus right? But Jesus preached every day, to loads of people, multitudes of people, so I reckon if Jesus preached so much, so loudly, everyday, he would have some serious throat problems. Check dis –
Surely it is good that football is played by the pure in heart,
For they who lose *not* their tempers may apply their minds wholly
unto the brilliant tackle,
And they that are chilled and calm
Shall be known as the chosen few,
They shall be called gifted,

Good guys,
And wicked strikers.
But yea I say unto ye
Those that bully and kick up man shin
Those that kick heels
Shall be burnt by their ill gained salty sweat
And many red cards will be in their midst,
Yea I say unto the spectators upon the terraces,
Those that are arrogant and loud mouthed shall fall upon the
unforgiving pitch
And dwell among the worms
And the spit of opposing defenders. *(Beat)*

That ain't the Bible or anything, that's just me messing about. But really, think about it, right, if Jesus played football he would have to be the captain because he was a leader of men, and that team would get no red cards. Actually, it would be even better if he was a referee, then he could bring the spirit of the Lord upon all the players before the game and the players would all respect each other – a bit like girls' football. *(Pause)*

I just went in the bathroom right, and I could see this towel – it had blood on it. Mom tried to hide it but I could see it. I hope it ain't gonna start up again.

6.

Off-stage, a group of kids are shouting abuse at Wali, outside school.

KIDS   Asylum creeper.
Can't even speak English.
Your Mom stinks.
You're a scrounger and a thief.
Hey, you look good in the dark.
You need some food aid.
Even your Dad thinks your Mom's ugly.

WALI *(shouting back)* Leave me alone, my English is better than yours. I got higher marks in English than any of you, so you should shut up.

Mark enters.

MARK   What's up Wali?

WALI   It's them lot, they're going on with all that
stupidness again.

MARK   Don't worry about them.

WALI   I don't worry about them, I was born a brummie, and
I'm still a brummie. I know that at least two of them lot are
foreigners. That boy there, him, the one who keeps calling me
asylum creeper, he comes from Nottingham. That's miles away.
And him the other one, the big one with the mash up nose, he
come from London, and he calls me a foreigner? Have you heard
the way he talks? They just jealous because I score more goals
than them.

MARK   Well, I won't call you any names but you can't score
more goals than me.

WALI   Yeah, I bet you're wrong, if that man from Aston
Villa saw me playing he would pick me before you, he only
picked you that day 'cause he didn't see me.

MARK   Yeah, yeah.

WALI   Yeah, you know it. Did you see football on the
television on Sunday?

MARK   No, there wasn't any.

WALI   There was... Afghanistan played, and guess what?
Afghanistan won. Three one.

MARK   I didn't see that, who did they play?

WALI   I can't remember now, some foreign team.

MARK   See, you don't even know who they played. No
offence guy but you gotta face the truth, no one's ever heard of
Afghanistan Football Club.

WALI   Just because you haven't that don't mean everyone
else hasn't, lots of people know about Afghanistan.

MARK   Listen guy, Afghanistan might have a couple of
good cricketers but I bet you can't name one famous Afghan
football player.

WALI   I can.

MARK	Go on then.
WALI	Em, em, what's his name now? Em, he's really famous but I can't remember his name now, but he's really good.
MARK	See you can't, and they're suppose to be your favourite team. OK then, how many other Afghanistan supporters are in our school?
WALI	Loads.
MARK	Loads?
WALI	Yeah loads, there's me, and Anwar, and Hamid.
MARK	That's amazing, there may even be four of you, gosh, that's great. I suppose if your parents come from Afghanistan you gonna support them. I supported Jamaica once, only for six weeks. But you gotta admit it, England ain't worried about Afghanistan, Brazil ain't worried about Afghanistan, Afghanistan have never, ever made it to the World Cup, and maybe they never, ever will.
WALI	Maybe they just can't be bothered, maybe they don't want to play in the World Cup. Who's world is it anyway?
MARK	I'll be in the World Cup before they are, one day I'll be there, you wait.
WALI	And you're gonna be the best poet in the world, as well?
MARK	Of course guy, but there's no such thing as the best poet. All poets are equal, but right now I'm reading as much poems as I can, and I'm reading loads when I'm not busy with me football. My plan is to write at least one poem every day, maybe more, but at least one.
WALI	Come on, what's so good about poetry? Poetry's not that important.
MARK	It is guy, poetry's bad. This is the way I see it right, I'm talking to you now, which is a bit like giving a part of meself to you.
WALI	Get off, I don't want a part of you.
MARK	Don't be silly, what I mean is I'm communicating with you, right? But then when I write a poem, and I read the poem back to meself, it's like communicating to meself, talking to meself.

WALI   I thought that when you start talking to yourself it means you're going mad.

MARK   Shut up, you know what I mean. Seriously guy, sometimes I say things that even surprise me. They're my poems, I write them, and I still get surprised. It's difficult to explain but poems help me to chill out and make me stronger.

WALI   I thought press-ups make you stronger.

MARK   Wali, stop messing.

WALI   I'm only joking, I know what you mean.

MARK   Anyway a poem a day, that's me ambition. You know what? From now on I think I'm only gonna share me poems with special people like me Mom.

WALI   Special?

MARK   Oh yes, and you of course, if you stop messing about.

Music.

7.

Mark in his room.

MARK   Wali's alright, he was born in the same hospital as me. People think he's soft but he ain't. His parents' house got bombed in Afghanistan, and his sister just disappeared, then his Mom and Dad had to walk for hundreds of miles to save their lives and his Mom was pregnant, then when they got here Wali was born. We're lucky in this country guy, at least we don't have to go through all that. *(Beat)* That Mrs. Macy meks me sick. Today I wanted to show her some of me poems but she doesn't even like poetry. She's getting the class to learn a poem right, and I had me own book of poems in me pocket to show her. So when she came to me, I said to her, 'Do you like poems, Miss?' and she said, 'No, not really Mark, but I have to teach poetry as part of English.' That's terrible innit? Just think if there was a Maths teacher that didn't like numbers, or a P.E. teacher that didn't like games. *(Beat)* Check dis. I didn't tell Wali but today I kissed Maria Shah. She said she would give me a kiss if I said a poem for her, so I made up something quickly in me head, nothing important, just a few lines.

I know a wicked girl
She's the best girl in the world,
Her name is Maria and I really love to see her,
And no matter where I see her guy I wanna drop a rhyme,
And when I drop a rhyme I mek her smile every time. *(Beat)*

She laughed, as she always does, and then she kissed me. She's alright but she tasted of baked beans guy. *(Pause)*
Better get some sleep now – school tomorrow.

Click. Lights out.

MARK   Good night.

In the darkness, sounds of struggle.

DAD   You will do what I say.

MOM   I will not.

DAD   You will do what I say because without me you'd starve, without me you are nothing. I keep you.

MOM   Typical man. Well, I'll get a job and keep myself.

DAD   Typical man, I'll give you typical man, if you don't shut it I'll slap ya.

MOM   That's you answer to everything ain't it. You have a low intelligence you know, you ain't got much upstairs.

DAD   What you saying?

MOM   Think about it.

DAD   I'm not joking, don't get me mad.

MOM   Oh shut up.

Light on Mark.

MARK *(whispering to himself while his parents argue)*

I know a wicked girl
She's the best girl in the world,
Her name is Maria and I really love to see her,
And no matter where I see her guy I wanna drop a rhyme,
And when I drop a rhyme I mek her smile everytime,
Smile everytime I mek her smile everytime
And when I drop a rhyme I mek her smile everytime.

Lights fade.

8. WEDNESDAY

Lights up. Wali is standing on platform/pulpit.

WALI   On the third day Mark did fifty press-ups, sixty
squats and sixty jumping jacks, and his fitness increaseth greatly.
And so it was on that day, in the safety of his own room, far from
any Birmingham City supporters, he did forty sit-ups, for sit-ups
maketh strong stomach muscles, and strong stomach muscles
bringeth forth an awesome six-pack. Then he looked down upon
his belly and he saw that it was cool.

*Wali jumps off the platform and joins Mark on the street, they start
kicking a ball around.*

MARK   Let's not go into school guy, let's wag it.

WALI   Shall we?

MARK   Yeah guy, don't worry, let's go to the corner shop
and nick some chocolates and crisps and stuff, and then we can
spend the whole day practising in the park. Me Mom won't know
because she doesn't really check up on me, and I left home at the
usual time anyway. I just can't be bothered guy. I don't mind the
lessons and that, but I hardly slept last night.

WALI   OK, too much school ain't good, that's what
someone told me. But why can't you sleep anyway?

MARK   Nothing. *(He pauses as he thinks about how to ask
the question.)* What do you do when your Dad hits your Mom?

WALI   He doesn't hit my Mom.

MARK   What do you mean, have you got one of them back to front family like what they preach about in church, is your Mom a feminist or something?

WALI   What are you going on about?

MARK   I'm just asking you what happens when your Dad hits your Mom.

WALI   And I just told you that he doesn't.

MARK   So what happens when your Mom hits your Dad?

WALI   Don't be silly, she doesn't hit my Dad. My parents don't hit each other.

MARK   You're lucky, guy.

WALI   If your parents are fighting you should talk to a teacher in school, or even a copper, because if your Dad's hitting your Mom he could be locked in the nick for it.

MARK   Your parents don't fight and they don't even go to church. I tell ya guy, just because you go to church that don't mean you're good, and some good people don't even go to church and they're cool. Your Parents don't go to church, do they, hey, do they?

WALI   No, well we don't have churches, we have mosques, but it the same thing really. Anyway, no, my parents don't go.

MARK   See, they don't go to church, or mosque, and they're cool.

WALI   Hey Mark, maybe we should go back to school?

MARK   No way, I'm not going there.

WALI   Look at them lot over there, so many of them, all wagging it.

MARK   Yeah look at them, they're gonna get caught 'cause they're so noisy, and they're puffin draw. I know a couple of them, they carry blades.

WALI   At least we're not carrying weapons or puffin weed.

MARK   Hey did you know that it was Aston Villa and a couple of other teams that started the first ever football league?

WALI   How do you know?

MARK   I know guy, I read about it. There's this letter right, it's still around today, and it's from the chairman or something of Aston Villa, to these other teams and it's saying let's get together and start a bit of a league. And most people think that football was invented in England right, but they had a kind of football game in China about four thousand years ago. They never had a proper ball; they just used a pig's bladder or something.

WALI   What, a pig's bladder, did they eat it afterwards?

MARK   Stop messing. Anyway, the first real ball was made in Mexico right, but it was some English people that made the rules up, and English people made the first proper pitches, so I suppose football is an English game.

WALI   I bet the Afghans did it really.

MARK   Yeah you would say that. Come on, pass me the ball, I gotta practise all me skills. Keeping the ball up, dribbling, you know, penalties and things like that. Mr Collins the P.E. teacher told me that there's gonna be loads of kids there, from different schools, so I gotta play good.

Music.

9.
Mark is in his room, reading.

MARK

What is the price of a baby?
A baby that will live long
A baby that will shine each day
Come what may.
It need not have a perfect father,
It need not have a perfect mother,
It need not be the son of a prince,
Or the daughter of a chosen one,
All it needs is the sweet smell of love
And a place that is sane and sheltered.
A beautiful smile once told me that
Babies need

But it's not about greed,
And I am so sure that smile would not lie.
So what is the price of a baby?
And do babies get cheaper the less they cry?

Lights change.
The parents' bedroom.

DAD   Doris, Doris, Doris, wake up – wake up.

MOM   What?

DAD   Get me some tea.

MOM   What?

DAD   Get me a cuppa tea.

MOM   What's the matter? Are you sick or something? Do you know what time it is?

DAD   I ain't sick, I just want a cup of tea, yeah. Now hurry up.

MOM   Come on, make it yourself. I'm tired man, I've been on me feet all day.

DAD   So you tired are you? You've been on your feet all day have you? And what about me? I've been running up and down in that damn warehouse like a madman all day. I'm the bloke that left this house at six-thirty this morning and never returned until seven this evening. I'm the one who's been on their feet all day, me, yeah me, the one who brings the money in this house. Your work ain't nothing compared to what I do. And if I didn't do it you wouldn't have a bed to sleep on.

MOM   So what you saying, you don't think I work?

DAD   That's right, you don't work, you can't call looking after children work, you're a woman, you're suppose to take these things in your stride. You're built for running the house, now get me cup of tea.

MOM   No, I've done my work for today, get it yourself.

DAD   I said get me some tea.

MOM   No.

DAD   I'm gonna tell you one more time, and only one
more time, get me some tea.

MOM   And I'll tell you one more time, no.

DAD   Look at that. What kind of wife are you? I ask you
for a cup of tea and look at the way you answer me.

MOM   Yes, well look at the way you treat me? I make your
breakfast, I prepare your clothes, make your lunch... When you
get home I put food on the table, if I can do all that I'm sure you
can do a simple thing like make yourself a cup of tea.

DAD   Shut up and get me tea.

MOM   No.

DAD   What?

MOM   No.

He slaps her. Baby cries.

MOM *(crying)* You see what you've done. Move from me.

DAD   You can't tell me to move, you should know that.
(He slaps her)

MOM   Take your hands off me, I can't take it any more
man, I'll fight you back.

DAD   You can't fight me you know. I run this house *(Slap)*
And ain't taking no nonsense from you
So just get your arse outta the bed and get me tea. *(Slap)*
If you got me tea in the first place then every ting
would be alright, ain't it? *(Slap)*
But you, you're a stubborn bitch *(Slap)*
You are a lazy, lazy slut *(Slap)*
If I could live my life again, you think I would marry you,
Not at all, because you are trash
You're Rubbish. You're nothing, you bitch... *(Slap)*

Mark, in his room, speaking over the beating to drown it out.

MARK   Wali's Dad took him to the pictures and the car
show in the summer holidays. I've never been to the pictures and

I'd love to go to a car show. He said there were hundreds of cars, new ones, old ones, cars that had three wheels, cars for the future that shouldn't need any petrol. Wish my Dad would take me.

Mom is now losing the fight.

MOM   Please leave me alone, I really can't take no more of this.

DAD   I don't done with you yet, whore. I gonna teach you some manners. When you talk to me you will talk to me with respect, you see. *(Slap)*
When I say move, you must move, you see.
You could read a million of those books about woman's rights. *(Slap)* In this house I'm the one who is right, you see. *(Slap)*

Mom is panting – losing breath.
Light on Mark. He speaks over them trying to blank it out.

MARK   Sometimes, I just don't care about you and your wars,
Sometimes I just don't care about you and the price of your food,
Sometimes I just want to beat the pain up
And kill the pressure,
Sometimes I just want to go and scream in church
Then fly home to make my very own Dad.

DAD   You better know your place right
You better have manners. *(Slap)*
When I tell you to do something, you do it.
When I say move, you move. *(Slap)*

MARK   Sometimes I just don't care about you and your money.
Sometimes I just don't care about you and your nice trainers
And your nice mobile phones, with your nice holders
and your nice covers.
Yes, that's right guy,

Sometimes I just don't care about your English and your Maths
And your present and your past,
Your Henry the Eighth, and your homework,
Sometimes I just don't care about you.
Sometimes I tell lies.
The truth is I care about everything, I love you Maria Shah,
But tonight, school is so unimportant,
And everything seems so loveless.

Dad is now standing over Mom.

DAD   Yes, now you know, don't try big up yourself with
me, I will damage you, you will get knock down quick. Look at
me a big working man, in me own home, all I want is some
service, a little tea, and you have to mek such a big ting out of it.
You must know now that you can't disobey me, you must know
now that I will not stand for any of your backchat. You know now
ain't it, you know now ain't it? *(Pause)* Now get me some tea.

MOM   No.

DAD   You living dangerously... I said, get me some tea.

MOM   No way, I'm no slave you know.

DAD   Right. *(Slap)* ...now what you saying?

MOM   You will burn in hell, that's what I'm saying, as
there is a god in heaven, you will burn in hell.

Dad takes a pillow and smothers her face.

MARK   Oh no, not again... *(crying)* ... he keeps suffocating
her or something, listen, she can't breathe, sounds like he's
strangling her... why does he keep doing it to her. *(Click. Lights
fade.)* Good night.

10. THURSDAY
Wali at platform/pulpit.

WALI   On the fourth day, Mark did sixty press-ups, sixty squats, sixty jumping jacks, sixty sit-ups and loads of running on the spot and his fitness increaseth greatly. And on that day many leg stretches were done and quick and supple limbs were created. And Mark looked, and behold, before him he saw an Aston Villa player of the future, a goal scorer of the highest order, poetry in motion, and he thought that that was wicked.

Mark is in his room, reading.

MARK

In this house that's falling down
We have two rooms,
One for us and one for the big people.
But the damp does not obey the rules
The damp lives in both rooms.

The damp hangs around the bathroom
Lingers in the kitchen
And watches over us like a dark menacing cloud
Waiting to explode.
The damp hugs this house; it seems to love this house.

This house is falling down
But it's still standing,
It has six rooms, three families
Two kitchens, one bathroom
And a garden that has outgrown
And disowned it.
Ants live here (I believe they speak)
Mice live here (I believe they speak)
Woodlice dine here (They speak with their mouths full)
But the damp expands silently
A shapeless body
A cold reminder of the outside.
I would love it if the wallpaper stayed on the walls,
I would love to know that no more plaster

Would fall upon my head or my bed.
But this is it,
The damp was here when we moved in
And it may still be here when this house is all over.
So don't knock it,
This house that's falling down
Is called my home.
(Pause)

Last night was horrible, must have been the worst night ever, I want it to stop guy, I really want it to stop, but I just hope that we don't have to run away again, I hate it when we run away, we shouldn't have to run. The thing is I like Birmingham, I like Aston, it's alright and they may not let me back into the school again. One time we ran away and we went to London and I hated it – so many people. The buses are packed, the trains are packed, even the schools are packed... no guy, I like it here, and it's so hard to mek friends there.

11.

Mark and Wali are kicking a football around on the streets.

MARK   Run to it.

WALI   Nice one, here you are, trap this and put it on me head.

MARK   Yes, look at that for a wicked pass.

WALI   Not bad. Now watch me, watch how many kick-ups I can do. One, two, three, four, five, six,

MARK   Not bad but, Wali I think one of them touched the ground.

WALI   Oh, you put me off, I was going for twenty. OK, I tell you what, let's do some headers.

MARK   OK.

WALI   I'll count... one, two, three, four, five, six. Mark man, we didn't even get to ten, you could have got that.

MARK   Sorry guy, I wasn't concentrating.

WALI   Yeah, you wasn't concentrating alright, that was an easy ball, anyone could have got that.

MARK   Alright, alright, don't rub it in.

They start to walk away.

WALI   You'll have to do better than that on Saturday, there's gonna be some good players down there.

MARK   Yeah yeah.

WALI   So how's Maria Shah then?

MARK   I don't know.

WALI   What do you mean you don't know, don't you like her any more?

MARK   She's cool, her birthday's coming up or something... I don't know, I just got other things to think about now innit.

WALI   What things, you worried about football trials?

MARK   Football trials are no problem guy, I just hope we ain't going away again.

WALI   Don't tell me that you're going to move away again?

MARK   I don't know. I don't know what's happening.

WALI   Find out man.

MARK *(raising his voice slightly)* I can't find out, how do you expect me to find out?

WALI   OK man, don't get angry with me, I'm supposed to be your best mate man, I'm only trying to help. I told you, if you got problems at home you can tell a teacher, tell Mr Aktar, that's what he's there for – family liaison officer or something like that, they call him. Or tell the coppers because dads have to behave as well, you know. I saw on the telly right, a programme about bad dads, and one of them went to jail.

MARK   OK, OK, you told me all that before.

WALI   You don't have to go away again.

MARK   I know, I know...

Music. They walk away.

12.

Mark sits on his bed.

MARK   Wali is me best friend, but he just don't know what's really going on. Everything would be alright if I get in that squad guy, it would be like a dream come true. I can't lose this chance. You should of seen me in school today, I played some wicked football. I'm serious, I was right on form, you should have seen me, I scored four goals and I helped set up two, so I know I can do it. *(Beat)* But I wish I could practise at home. The family downstairs got that big garden to themselves but they can't use it because of the neighbours. I would use it anyway – I don't care if they call me black, I'll call them white. A garden would be so cool guy. I hate this house. Mom said that one day we'll live in a whole house instead of a silly little flat and we'll have our own bathroom. Carlton won't have to sleep with Mom and Dad, and I won't have to sleep in the same room as a girl. I want a garden guy, to practise me skills. *(Beat)* And guess what? Maria Shah said that I can go to her birthday party next week. She hasn't even invited Wali, only me. And I was told that most of the kids there will be girls, only a few special boys are going and I'm one of them. Well, she keeps asking me to read poems to her innit? 'Cause I mek her laugh all the time. She's always watching me when I'm playing football, now she wants me to go to her party, she likes me innit, yeah guy she wants me badly. She smells like baked beans but I still like her, but I ain't going to tell her that, am I? Anyway I think football's more important now. *(Beat)* Me Mom, that's who I really love. I know hundreds of kids say that about their Moms and everyone thinks their Mom's special but my Mom is. She ain't perfect. No one's perfect, but she's tough and she sticks by me, innit?

Tap on door, Mom enters the room, which is dark.

MOM   It's alright son, it's only me.

MARK   Turn the light on Mom.

MOM   No, leave it off for now. I can see.

MARK	Mom, what's the matter, are you alright?
MOM	Never mind, everything will be alright so don't worry yourself.
MARK	Mom, are we going to go away again?
MOM	Angela sleeping?
MARK	Yes.
MOM	Good.
MARK	That's all she does. Mom, are we going away again or what?
MOM	Don't you worry, we will soon be gone.
MARK	No Mom, no, we can't go... what about me football trials? I can't miss them, this is me chance to show off me skills, this is me chance to actually play at Villa Park, I can't miss that Mom... we can't go, where we going anyway?
MOM	Don't worry... *(kiss)* ...it's him, he will soon be gone.

She leaves.

MARK *(to audience)* Did you see my Mom's face? Did you see it? Even in the dark I could see... You could see it, all puffed up with loads of bruises... It's the worst guy, I feel bad, I feel angry guy. I hate me Dad. He thinks he's good because he goes to work and his boss likes him, and in church all the people say, 'Brother Campbell, you preach so good.' But you see my Mom's face, that ain't done by a good person. It's people like me Dad who give God a bad name. *(Beat)* Angela wet the bed last night. It's a good job we got different beds now.

Lights fade.

13. FRIDAY
Wali at the platform/pulpit.

WALI　　　On the fifth day, Mark did even more press-ups, and even more squats, jumping jacks, sit-ups and running on the spot. And his six-pack shone in all its muscular glory, and his upper body strength was tops, and he looked and he smiled for he knew that he had created a bad footballing machine, capable of two hat-tricks in ninety minutes. All was good, it was brilliant I say unto thee, he was up for it, he felt well nice. Then he said unto himself...

Light on Mark, in his room.

MARK *(shouts)* Go forth and score. *(speaking quickly – excited as he shows off his books)* Yes. Wicked. Check this out, this one's poetry, and this one's football. This one's called 'Oh My Word' and it's lots of short poems and raps by different poets. Fun poems you know, word play and stuff like that. And this one, well it's easy ain't it? 'The Complete Encyclopaedia of Aston Villa'. Brilliant or what? I said I would do it and now this is serious, I'm gonna start me own little library. Mom said if I look after these I could get more when she can afford it. Not bad hey? And I wasn't even expecting anything. This is what happened right. We were coming from school, Mom was doing her shopping, Carlton was in his pushchair, Angela was there, talking, talking, talking. Then we stopped to buy some vegetables and then after that I saw right in front of me, in the window of a bookshop, this book, the poetry one. Because I got it from the library before I knew it was really funny so I said to me Mom that one day I'll get me own copy of that. Then we went into the bookshop and we started just looking around and Mom saw this book she liked about Jamaica, and then I saw this big Villa book. So I started looking at the pictures and me Mom came up to me and said do I really want a book to take home, and I said yes, and she said which one and I said, 'Boy it's so hard to choose.' Then she went away, in a corner like, and I saw her looking in her purse and counting all her money and then, guess what? She came back and said I could have both, I couldn't believe it guy, both of them. And then guess what? She bought a book about horses for Angela, and she bought that book about Jamaica for herself. Look at that man, I can't believe it, brand new, don't mess, and I don't even have to take it back to the library. *(Beat)* You wait, it's gonna happen, guy. One day you'll see me in the paper, Mark Anthony Campbell, footballer and poet, so watch out. I ain't showing off or anything, I just know what I know. Me poems are gonna make people laugh and cry, they're gonna be like intelligent poems that make people think about things going on in the world. And maybe I'll get meself a big house like Aston Hall, you know those types of houses that have a long drive and a garden like a park, that kind of house. And if I get married, I might marry a poet, yes guy, a poet wife for a poet husband... I wonder if Maria Shah is really a poet. Anyway check this out, I had this idea right, we could even have a poet priest to marry us, so he could say something like: 'Do you take this poet as your lawful wedded wife? Do you want to live with her for all your life? She's cool and she's wicked and she's standing at your side, So do it poet, drop a rhyme and kiss your lovely bride.' *(slowing down the pace)* But I tell you what, I wouldn't hit her. I wouldn't marry someone and then beat them up, what's that for? Why marry someone and then spend so much time beating them up? If I really get upset and lose me temper, I'll just go for a walk or write a poem. I'd just say, 'We must talk dis ting over Maria,' and then we would talk about it, you know what I mean? If Angela had a husband and he hit her I would fight him but that's different ain't it? That's helping Angela, defending me sister but I ain't gonna be no wife-beater.

Mark walks into his parents' room.

MARK　　　　Hey Dad, look at me book, it's all about Aston Villa, it ain't half good.

DAD　　　　Yes.

MARK　　　　Do you wanna have a look?

DAD　　　　No.

MARK　　　　I got another one here – poems.

DAD　　　　Where did you get them from?

MARK　　　　Mom bought them for us today, in town. Do ya wanna have a look?

DAD　　　　No. Go to your bedroom.

MARK　　　　Dad, if you like, we can share them, me and you.

DAD   I said go to your bedroom, now.

Mark goes back to his room.

MOM *(playing with baby Carlton)* How come you so pretty, boy? How come you so handsome? You already have all the little baby girls after you. Everybody loves my baby, everybody wants to hug my baby.

DAD *(interrupting)* Where did you get money from to waste on them books?

MOM   I got the money from me purse, innit.

DAD   What do you mean, money in your purse? What money in your purse? Where did it come from?

MOM   What kind of stupid question is that? It's me spending money, money from my purse.

DAD   Since when have you had spending money? The money I give you, is money for food and housekeeping – I never give you money to buy books. We send kids to school to read books. Make the government buy them books, make the education people give them books, the government take plenty tax money from me for books. Right now I'm working hard to put food on the table and to pay rent, and you want buy books. Tell me, how much money have you spend on that book rubbish?

MOM   Never you mind how much.

DAD   I said tell me how much?

MOM   And I said never you mind how much.

DAD *(really shouting)* Listen bitch, I work damn hard for you and these kids, that bloody warehouse has put me in hospital, money don't come easy, so you tell me how much of my money have you spent on stupid, ungodly books.

MOM *(shouting)* Twenty-five pounds.

DAD *(shouting)* Twenty-five pounds.

MOM *(shouting)* What – you deaf? I said, twenty-five pounds.

He slaps her. She screams.

DAD   Who the hell told you to spend twenty-five quid on rubbish when we don't even have money to pay the electric bill right now? What do you think I'm made of – money?

He slaps her. She screams.

DAD   Take those books back. Take the stupid things back and get the money back... I'll show you how to spend it.

MOM *(screaming hysterically)* I not taking nothing back. Leave me alone. Get your hands off me, you nasty dog, move, leave me alone. Who do you think you are? Who the hell do you think you are?

DAD   I know who I am, I run tings. I pay for everything in this house. Me? I'm the man.

MOM   So what kind of man are you? What kind of man likes to hit women in their face? I'm warning you, if you touch me again I will hit you back, I ain't scared of you.

DAD   Alright, come bitch. *(Slap)*

MOM   There. *(She hits him)*

DAD   I told you, the next time you try fight me back... gonna beat you so hard, your own mother wouldn't recognise you. *(Slap)*

MOM *(loud scream)* Leave me alone... *(shouting and fighting)* Leave me alone. Who do you think you are?

DAD   I tell you, and this time I gonna teach you a lesson for good... *(Slap)* You're a tramp... *(Slap)* You think me, a grown man can take backchat from you? *(Slap)* You think you can just spend my money as you please? *(Slap)* Don't you know that if a man can't control his woman he's not a – *(Slap)* man. *(Slap)* So this is me, in control. *(Slap. Slap. Slap. Slap. Slap. Slap.)*

MOM   You won't get away with this, as there is a god up in heaven, you will not get away with this.

Sound of fighting back and baby crying.
Mark is in his room, reading.

MARK

Soon we will live quite happily
Me and my little family,
Yes soon this house that we call home
Will sigh in sweet relief.
The bad vibrations will be gone.
And joy and love will know my Mom,
And all that noise that we have known
Will just melt into peace.
My books will sit upon their shelves
All getting to know themselves,
And Angela and Carlton
Will be very young and free.
Yes, peace will come and stay with us
And surely there will be no fuss,
A house where people do not cuss?
But where will Daddy be?

Click. Lights fade.

MARK   Good night.

14. SATURDAY

Wali is at the platform / pulpit. Mark is in the wardrobe.

WALI   And on the sixth day everything got messed up.
Wickedness happened. That's about it really, it's not good,
I tell ya.

MARK   No football, no bloody football. All that training for
nothing. All that hard work for nothing. *(Beat)*
I don't care about me Dad. Last night when he was hitting me
Mom I wanted to stop him, I wanted to fight him, I wanted to do
him in. I was fed up of hearing me Mom crying. I told Angela to
get in here with me. So we both sat here, and we put these
trousers and dresses and blankets over our heads so that we
couldn't hear what was going on, but we could still hear it, it was
horrible guy. We could hear Carlton crying his eyes out. You

wouldn't like it, none of you would like it. And last night I had a horrible dream as well – a nightmare kind of dream. I dreamt that fighting was everywhere. People were fighting in the house; the people in the downstairs flat were fighting, when I looked outside all the people in the streets were fighting. It was like the whole world had gone to war. But not with guns, just hands, slapping and punching each other. People fighting everywhere, and all love poems or anything that was good was being burnt. We're all messed up guy, that's what can happen when you listen to your parents fighting all the time. And look now, no football, and police all over the house, just 'cause of him. I ain't coming out of here, they'll have to come and get me, this wardrobe is the safest place in this house, those adults better sort themselves out. *(Beat)* I'll tell you something, me Dad could have been a good Dad but he didn't think... he thought about his food, his sleep, his work, and his this, that and the other, but he didn't think about us. I tried to love him but he didn't have no time for me. You know something, he never ever read one of me poems, not one, and he never ever watch me play football. He never loved me, so why should I love him? He made me Mom frightened and terrified all the time, yeah, that's real terrorism. *(Beat)*
I know that not all men are like him, and I don't want to be anything like him when I grow up. *(Beat)*
That's why I've got to keep writing me poetry and playing football, 'cause I wanna be the best ever, I wanna be like a legendary footballing poet, famous for scoring boss goals and doing good things. When they write the book of 'The History of Aston Villa'; I wanna be in it. *(Beat)* My Dad, he just couldn't stop hitting me Mom and treating her horrible. It's like this, right – me Dad didn't care about us, he didn't care about us kids, and he didn't care about me Mom.
(Pause)
That's why me Mom ... killed me Dad.

Lights fade to black.

The end.

Benjamin Zephaniah

Born in Handsworth, Birmingham. His poetry is strongly influenced by the music and poetry of Jamaica. *Page One Books* published his first book *Pen Rhythm*, when he was 22, and since then he has written 7 plays, 7 books for adults and 5 books for children, as well as performing his poetry, acting and presenting on radio, television and the stage. His plays include: *Playing the Right Tune* (1985), *Job Rocking* (1987), *Delirium* (1987), *Streetwise* (1990), *Mickey Tekka* (1991) Radio: *Hurricane Dub* won the BBC's Young Playwright's Award (1989) *Our Teachers Gone Crazy* (1990), TV: *Dread Poets Society,* BBC (1991) His poetry and novels include: *Talking Turkeys* (Puffin/Penguin), *Funky Chickens* (Puffin/Penguin), *Wicked World* (Puffin/Penguin), *Face* (Bloomsbury), *Refugee Boy* (Bloomsbury)

Precious

Precious

In writing *Precious,* I wanted to consider the choices we make at particular stages of our lives and the influences, subtle and overt, which lead us to making those choices. I wanted to explore the self-fulfilling prophecy and the possibility of breaking away from what is expected of us.

Precious' story can also be viewed in a wider context. As a young black woman, she is living out the personal and emotional consequences of recent history – post-war immigration to Britain, colonialism and, ultimately, slavery. These factors, I believe, still have a significant influence on our society today.

Angela Turvey

Precious

Angela Turvey

First performed at Windsor Arts Centre on 25th September, 2003.
Directed by Rosamunde Hutt, designed by Jane Mackintosh.
Lighting designed by Ceri James.

PRECIOUS 17, British, Jamaican parentage **Natasha Narcisse**
KAMALA 17, British, Indian parentage **Mina Barber**
WOMAN 37, British, Jamaican parentage **Maxine Finch**

Company Stage Manager – Beth Hoare
Associate Artist – Bernadette O'Brien
Movement Director – Chix Chandaria
Composer – Errollyn Wallen
Accent Advice – Jan Haydn Rowles
Casting – Bernadette O'Brien
Dramaturge – Bonnie Greer
Education Resources – Michael Judge
Production Manager – Marijke Zwart
Production Assistant – Joseph Coelho
Set Builder – Arcangel
Graphic Design – Iain Lanyon
Production Photography – Hugo Glendinning

With thanks to: Debbie Stubbs and colleagues at Windsor Arts Centre; Mina Barber, Nicole Davies, and Angela Michaels for their work on the development of the script; teachers and students at Baylis Court School in Slough; the team at Creative Partnerships – Slough.

Note: The play is set in a suburban town in Britain.

Precious' Song
In the original production, Precious' song used the words of a
Traditional Afro-Amercian Spiritual (with new music by Errollyn
Wallen available via Theatre Centre.)

I'm a stranger, stranger here;
I'm a stranger, everywhere.
Lord you know I would go home,
Lord you know I would go home –
but I'm a stranger here.

I'd rather drink muddy water,
I'd rather sleep on a hollow log,
Than to stay in this city, stay in this city
Being treated like a dirty dog.
I'm a stranger...

1.
The streets of a suburban town. Clusters of square, white houses
appear to shoot out of the ground. Despite variations in size and
detail, the overall impression is of uniformity.
Graffiti on the wall – the tag 'POW'. In the background, music
pulses – a party. Woman enters. Her eyes are drawn to the tag. A
modern bhangra hit plays. Woman smiles to herself thoughtfully as
police sirens begin to sound in the distance.

PRECIOUS *(Off)* Run!
KAMALA *(Off)* I'm running.

Woman exits. Precious and Kamala run on, fear and excitement on
their faces. Each carries a rucksack.

PRECIOUS   Come on!
KAMALA   Alright!
PRECIOUS   Quickly!

They crouch behind a wall. Eventually, Precious emerges.

PRECIOUS   They've gone.

Kamala drags her back.

KAMALA   Wait!

They both emerge slowly.

PRECIOUS   They went the other way.
KAMALA   Shhh!
PRECIOUS   For goodness sake!
KAMALA   There were two of them.
PRECIOUS   So?
KAMALA   I saw one turn off.
PRECIOUS   They both turned off.
KAMALA   You weren't looking.
PRECIOUS   Kamala, just relax. They've gone, OK?
KAMALA   They saw us.
PRECIOUS   They saw two people running away.
KAMALA   Well, they'll know it's us.
PRECIOUS   How?
KAMALA   Like we're not the only brown faces 'round here.
Mum and Dad are going to freak. *(Precious pulls a face, mocking
her.)* It's a criminal offence.
PRECIOUS *(Mock horror)* We could go to prison!
KAMALA   We could.
PRECIOUS   For painting a wall?
KAMALA   It's illegal.
PRECIOUS   I'm so scared!
KAMALA   You'd tell them, wouldn't you Precious? You'd tell
them it's not me. You would, wouldn't you?
PRECIOUS   Yes Kamala, I'll tell them.

Kamala looks around.

KAMALA   Where are we?
PRECIOUS   End of the high street – the new houses. It's called 'The Spinneys' now.
KAMALA   What was here before?
PRECIOUS   A gap.

Kamala sees the tag.

KAMALA   So you've already done this place?
PRECIOUS   Look – they've tried to rub it off.
KAMALA *(sarcastic)* Oh no! *(Precious takes spray cans from her rucksack)* Precious!
PRECIOUS   Just touching it up.

Precious starts to re-spray her tag.

KAMALA   Haven't you done enough today? What if the police come back?
PRECIOUS   They won't.

Kamala looks around anxiously.

KAMALA   These places have security guards – dogs sometimes. I hate dogs.
PRECIOUS   Give me the rest of the cans.

Kamala takes off her rucksack and hands it to Precious.

KAMALA   Just hurry up.
PRECIOUS   You don't have to stay.
KAMALA *(considers)* Is this your last one?
PRECIOUS   Probably. Yes.

Kamala sits down.

KAMALA   People are really angry about this, you know? Makes the town look like a ghetto, that's what they're saying. They come into the shop and tell us how they spend the weekend scrubbing walls. It was front page news in '*The Echo*' last week – 'Rid Our Town of Graffiti Menace' – and a picture of *your* tag.

PRECIOUS   Where?

KAMALA   By the station.

PRECIOUS   Good one that.

KAMALA   You don't care, do you?

PRECIOUS *(laughs)* Your face!

KAMALA   This is serious, Precious. We're in big trouble.

PRECIOUS   Got to catch us first.

KAMALA   If I'd known you were out tagging... Your Mum said you'd gone into town.

PRECIOUS   I did – to go tagging.

KAMALA   Does she know it's you?

PRECIOUS   'Course not. Can you imagine it? 'You bring shame on this house!' *(Beat)* You know what Kamala, you didn't have to come looking for me.

KAMALA   I've not seen you since school finished. I thought we could catch up.

PRECIOUS   I've called round.

KAMALA   I've been helping in the shop. I told you.

PRECIOUS   You spent half the summer in Southall.

KAMALA   Staying with my cousin. I had that dancing competition.

PRECIOUS   Oh yeah – how did you do?

KAMALA   Second.

PRECIOUS   Not bad.

KAMALA   Everyone said I should have won.

PRECIOUS   The holiday's flown by.

KAMALA   Well, we'll be seeing each other every day soon.

PRECIOUS   Will we?

KAMALA   When we go back to school.
PRECIOUS   I'm not going back to school.
KAMALA   What?
PRECIOUS   I was going to tell you.
KAMALA   But... we've got to go back, retake our exams, get
good grades.
PRECIOUS   I haven't got to do anything.
KAMALA   What about your Mum and Dad?
PRECIOUS   What about them?
KAMALA   They want you to re-sit, don't they?
PRECIOUS   They've never actually asked me what I want.
KAMALA   So what are you going to do?
PRECIOUS   Dunno.
KAMALA   You've got to have a plan.
PRECIOUS   Have I?
KAMALA   That's what Dad says.
PRECIOUS   And that's why you're going back? Because your
Dad says you've got to?
KAMALA   No. I want to go back.
PRECIOUS   Well, I don't.
KAMALA   You'll end up like Julie Wilson if you're not careful
– screwing on bottle tops in the *Fizzyade* factory. That's what
happens to people who don't pass their exams.
PRECIOUS   Says who?
KAMALA   It's a well-known fact. You need five passes for
university or a decent job.
PRECIOUS   And what's a decent job? Pen-pushing in an office?
KAMALA   It's what your Dad does.
PRECIOUS   It's what he chose to do – what everyone 'round here
chooses to do. Not me.
KAMALA   You have to re-take your exams Precious.
PRECIOUS   Why?
KAMALA   Because... you're clever and if you hadn't spent half
your time doing this. *(Kamala gets to her feet and idly goes*

through some dance steps.) Well, I'm going back. If I put my
mind to it, I could do law or medicine. I could.

PRECIOUS Good luck to you.

KAMALA What does that mean?

PRECIOUS Touchy.

KAMALA So what *are* you going to do instead?

PRECIOUS I'm going to get out of here. Travel the world.

KAMALA On your own?

PRECIOUS You could come.

KAMALA Me?

PRECIOUS Why not?

KAMALA Because –

Precious stops what she is doing to talk to Kamala.

PRECIOUS We could go to exotic countries, like we've seen in
our geography books, places where the sun shines all the time,
where there's light and colour, not like here. We'd meet all kinds
of people – spend our days lying on the beach...

KAMALA Swimming, scuba diving...

PRECIOUS Fishing, sailing...

PRECIOUS We could go to Jamaica.

KAMALA Via India.

PRECIOUS Of course. Stay with relatives.

KAMALA Aunts.

PRECIOUS Cousins.

KAMALA Uncles.

PRECIOUS We might end up living out there.

KAMALA Where?

PRECIOUS I dunno. Somewhere. Somewhere where we would
just blend in.

KAMALA And when you say your name, they don't say,
'What? Pamela? Camilla?'

PRECIOUS   'Precious? What a funny name. Who called *you*
Precious?' *(Beat)*
KAMALA   Can you see my parents letting me go round the
world? I'm just about allowed down the high street on my own.

Precious continues to work on her tag.

PRECIOUS   Well I'm not staying here. Boring, faceless town,
blank walls, blank people, blank faces.
KAMALA   Leaving your mark, though.
PRECIOUS   In some countries, they pay artists to do this.
KAMALA   Yeah!

Kamala spots someone in the distance.

KAMALA   Who's that?
PRECIOUS   Where?
KAMALA   Someone's coming.
PRECIOUS   Just some old bloke.
KAMALA   A security guard!
PRECIOUS   No.
KAMALA   Yes!
PRECIOUS   Put the cans in here.

*They stuff their rucksacks with the spray cans. Sound of dogs
barking.*

KAMALA   I told you – dogs.

*The barking stops – they freeze. It starts again, much louder and
closer. They see the funny side.*

PRECIOUS   Run! *(They run off, laughing.)*

2.

We see a room in Precious' house and a room in Kamala's house simultaneously. In Precious' house, muffled sounds of a television come from another room. Precious enters carrying her rucksack, her hands covered in paint.

PRECIOUS *(calls)* Only me. *(She takes off the rucksack and washes her hands, scrubbing furiously at the paint.)* Just went for a walk – on my own. To clear my head. *(Beat)* Dad? Why did you call me Precious? Kamala and I were talking about it the other day and I thought – why Precious? Am I named after somebody? Was it Grandma's idea? *(Beat)* Dad? *(She dries her hands.)* Are you listening to me?

An urgent, musical fanfare heralds the beginning of the television news. Kamala runs into the room at her house. She searches through a pile of newspapers and pulls out a copy of 'The Echo'.

KAMALA Here it is.

Precious takes the spray cans out of her rucksack and arranges them carefully in front of her. Kamala reads from 'The Echo' as Big Ben strikes between each phrase:

KAMALA Graffiti vandal strikes again – residents fear surge in youth crime – latest victim says, 'Where will it all end?' – Police say a suspect has been arrested.

She looks over anxiously at Precious. Having arranged the cans neatly, Precious sweeps them into a bin. She sings her song. Lights fade.

3.

Precious scrubs at graffiti on a wall. Woman enters not noticing her. She takes a packet of cigarettes from her bag, pulls one out and contemplates lighting it. Eventually, she throws it to the ground and crushes it underfoot.

PRECIOUS   I would have had that.

WOMAN   Precious?

PRECIOUS   Got any more?

WOMAN   I don't know why I bought them. I gave up. Years ago.

PRECIOUS   Looks like it! Nervous, were you? Meeting a tearaway like me? I could pull a knife.

WOMAN   What are you doing?

PRECIOUS   What does it look like? I've been a bad girl.

WOMAN   Have you?

PRECIOUS   What's it to you? I know your type. Volunteers with too much time on their hands.

WOMAN   Not me.

PRECIOUS   A 'mentor' then, sent to save me from myself. You could give me a hand with this.

WOMAN   No way.

PRECIOUS   Get lost, then.

WOMAN   I quite like it as it is.

PRECIOUS   You what –?

WOMAN   I like it.

PRECIOUS   Do you?

WOMAN   I think it's great – colour, energy, passion. I'm probably not supposed to say that. *(Beat)*

PRECIOUS   I'm famous. Everyone knows me. 'See her, she'll come to nothing – end up wasting her life.' That's what they want, the self-fulfilling prophecy – becoming what they say I am – a waster, a vandal. But vandals destroy things, don't they? I don't destroy anything. I just... make my mark.

WOMAN   What was there before?

PRECIOUS   A blank wall.

WOMAN   Then that's definitely an improvement.

PRECIOUS   It is, isn't it?

WOMAN	I paint a bit myself.
PRECIOUS	Do you? What? Painting and decorating?
WOMAN	No.
PRECIOUS	You're an artist? A real artist?
WOMAN	Amongst other things.
PRECIOUS	I've never met an artist before. *(returning to her sour mood)* Is that why you're here? To be a 'positive influence'?
WOMAN	A friend – hopefully. There's an exhibition at the local gallery. We could go and see it. Might be interesting. *(Beat)*
PRECIOUS	I hate this town. Hate it.
WOMAN	It's your home.
PRECIOUS	Mum and Dad's home, not mine. Not for much longer.
WOMAN	You've got plans?
PRECIOUS	You bet I've got plans. I'm going away.
WOMAN	Where to?
PRECIOUS	Just away, out of here. You wouldn't understand. You've probably got a nice comfortable life somewhere – husband, family...
WOMAN	You shouldn't make assumptions about people. They're rarely what they seem. You should know that more than anybody. *(Beat)*
PRECIOUS	I've let them down – Mum and Dad. But I don't care. They just worry what the neighbours think. They're not bothered about me. Toe the line, keep your head down, set an example. They've certainly let me know what a disappointment I am.
WOMAN	Parents are all the same. I don't think my Dad ever forgave me for not becoming an accountant – because that's a proper job, you know.
PRECIOUS	That's what mine keep saying. What *is* a proper job?
WOMAN	Exactly.
TOGETHER	They just don't understand.

They laugh. Precious goes back to her cleaning.

PRECIOUS   I've seen it all before, you know. You don't fool me.
WOMAN   What do you mean?
PRECIOUS   All this sidling up, trying to 'make a connection'.
WOMAN   I'm just talking to you.
PRECIOUS   Someone I can look up to.
WOMAN   I should be. Don't know if I am. *(Beat)* I want to get
away sometimes.
PRECIOUS   You?
WOMAN   Escape.
PRECIOUS   From what?

Precious hums a phrase of her song and exits.

WOMAN   It starts off like any other day – the sun makes its
way through a clear blue sky, the faintest chill in the wind
reminds me it's nearly autumn. I'm early for my appointment.
The doctor comes in, sits down – and I think it strange that he
doesn't look me in the eye. I have the results of the tests, he says
and there is no easy way to tell you this. The words fall out of his
mouth, jumble together, don't make sense. Slowly, I understand. I
will never be a mother. I will never know what it's like to hold
my own baby in my arms. I will never experience that love, the
love of a mother for her child. Never. I don't go back to the
studio. I haven't worked since. The sky is ice blue and a weak,
faded sun gives no warmth. Summer has disappeared.

4.
*Precious' bedroom. Precious is in front of a mirror putting on make
up. In the background, sounds of television canned laughter. A knock
at the door. Kamala enters dressed in traditional clothes.*

PRECIOUS   At last! *(She ushers her in and closes the door.)*
We're going out.
KAMALA   Where?
PRECIOUS   To a party.
KAMALA   You didn't say on the 'phone.

PRECIOUS	Mum and Dad were listening.
KAMALA	We can't go to a party. You're grounded.
PRECIOUS	They can't ground me.
KAMALA	Precious...
PRECIOUS	I'm going.
KAMALA	You'll just make things worse for yourself.
PRECIOUS	And you're coming with me.
KAMALA	Who's party is it?
PRECIOUS	Lucy's brother... a friend of his.
KAMALA	You don't even know them.
PRECIOUS	Steve's going to be there.
KAMALA	Steve? So you *do* like him?
PRECIOUS	'Course I like him.
KAMALA	But you ignore him.

PRECIOUS *Because* I like him. You have got so much to learn. Anyway, I think it's about time he knew I'm interested – and tonight's the night.

KAMALA What if he's not there?

PRECIOUS It'll be a laugh anyway. We'll dance the night away, have fun. Anything's better than these four walls.

KAMALA I'm not going without a proper invitation.

PRECIOUS A proper invitation? What? Written on parchment and delivered by a footman?

WOMAN I'm not like you.

PRECIOUS Meaning?

KAMALA You're in enough trouble, Precious.

PRECIOUS I'm not spending another night in this room, OK? Here. *(She holds out a make-up bag to Kamala.)* They're my colours but some might suit you. *(Kamala refuses to take it.)* Come on, Kamala. I'm tearing my hair out. If it's no good, we'll come straight back. Promise.

After some thought, Kamala takes the bag.

KAMALA I can't be too late.

PRECIOUS   I know.

Kamala joins Precious at the mirror.

KAMALA   How will we get out without your parents noticing?

PRECIOUS   You'll see.

KAMALA   And if we get caught?

PRECIOUS   We won't.

KAMALA   You are...

PRECIOUS   Stupid? Mad?

KAMALA   I was going to say brave. *(Precious puts on bhangra music which drowns the noise of the television.)* You've still got this?

PRECIOUS   I love it. Good memories. Miss Taylor's PE class, Monday morning.

KAMALA   Why did I agree to that? It was your fault. You told her I took dance lessons. *(mimicking)* 'Why don't you show us a few moves, Kamala. A little routine, maybe.' One lesson she didn't have to plan.

PRECIOUS   I thought it was great.

KAMALA   The boys didn't.

PRECIOUS   We had to do football – they shouldn't moan about a bit of dance.

KAMALA   They threatened to beat me up.

PRECIOUS   No!

KAMALA   Didn't I tell you? I got out of school early and ran home.

PRECIOUS   So what's Miss Taylor up to this term?

KAMALA   I don't know. I didn't go back to school, Precious.

PRECIOUS   I thought... what about your plan? *(Kamala shrugs.)* So you can come with me – around the world?

KAMALA   Dad's got other ideas.

PRECIOUS   Who's life is it exactly?

KAMALA   Mum and Dad want the best for me, OK?

PRECIOUS   OK. *(Precious sees that Kamala is upset. She turns the music up and starts to dance.)* Come on! You remember. *(Precious dances, encouraging Kamala to her feet. They dance together enjoying the music, the memory and each other's company. Eventually they slump down, exhausted.)* The time!

KAMALA   You can't be late for a party.

PRECIOUS   Yes you can. The food's gone, the drinks gone or the good-looking guys are taken.

KAMALA   Well, I don't drink, I'm not hungry... and I've got a man.

PRECIOUS   You what?

KAMALA   There's this friend of my Dad's, he's got a son. They thought we'd get on, you know. We went there tonight. That's why I was late.

PRECIOUS   Oh...

KAMALA   Nothing's definite.

PRECIOUS   But–?

KAMALA   Could be –

PRECIOUS   Marriage? *(Kamala nods)* Where will you live? The Spinneys?

KAMALA   America.

PRECIOUS   America?

KAMALA   But nothing's been decided, not yet.

PRECIOUS   America! So what's he like, this...

KAMALA   Anil? He's alright. He's nice.

PRECIOUS   Do you fancy him?

KAMALA   Mmmm...

PRECIOUS   Yes or no?

KAMALA   It's not a matter of yes or no.

PRECIOUS   No then.

KAMALA   He's OK.

PRECIOUS   OK? You're going to have sex with him, Kamala. A stranger. You've got to fancy him a bit otherwise it'll be... *(she shivers)*... ugh!

KAMALA   Stop it, Precious.

PRECIOUS   I'm just saying –

KAMALA   Oh, it's OK. I was thinking the same myself. In fact I've thought about nothing else since we got back. Do you remember Cathy Brown? She used to do it with anybody – strangers, passing lorry drivers –

PRECIOUS   And boast about it.

KAMALA   She didn't care, did she?

PRECIOUS   Couldn't give a monkey's... *(Beat)*

KAMALA   I think I always imagined I'd have some say in it – because they're reasonable people, Mum and Dad. And I've always known this is how my life will be.

PRECIOUS   What about university?

KAMALA   I can do things the other way round – get married first, have children...

PRECIOUS   Children?

KAMALA   Why not? Everyone wants kids, don't they?

PRECIOUS   No way. I've got too much planned for my life.

KAMALA *(hint of sarcasm)* Have you?

PRECIOUS   I certainly have.

KAMALA   You say that, but you never actually do anything, do you Precious?

PRECIOUS   What do you mean?

KAMALA   You keep saying you're going round the world.

PRECIOUS   Yeah?

KAMALA   Well, you need money.

PRECIOUS   I'll work my way round.

KAMALA   You need your fare to start with.

PRECIOUS   I'm looking for a job – Mum! What's the matter with you?

KAMALA   You criticise my life and you're just stuck here doing nothing. You don't even know what you want.

PRECIOUS   I wasn't criticising, Kamala. I'm on your side.

KAMALA   I know. It's just sometimes, things seem to be moving really fast and it's like I can't keep up.

They finish their make-up.

PRECIOUS   Are you ready?
KAMALA   Yep.
PRECIOUS   OK... Back door.
KAMALA   Are you sure about this?
PRECIOUS   Just have to turn the music up. *(She does so)*
Come on. We're going to have some fun.

Exit Kamala and Precious.

5.

Kamala reads from the newspaper.

KAMALA   To the Editor from Reginald Froggat, number nine
The Birches – Dear Sir, our beautiful town continues to be
afflicted by the menace of graffiti. Despite constant assurances,
the ten foot mural on my boundary wall has still not been
removed. How sad to see our town and its characteristic white-
washed walls blighted in this way.

6.

*An art gallery. Large, abstract paintings. Woman sits on a bench.
Precious enters.*

WOMAN   There you are! I was just about to go.
PRECIOUS   I'm here now.
WOMAN   An hour late. You're wasting my time.
PRECIOUS   I was busy.
WOMAN   And I'm not? I don't have to do this, you know.
PRECIOUS   I know.
WOMAN   I thought it might be something you'd enjoy. I'm in
no mood for it now. *(She turns to go.)*
PRECIOUS   Sorry. I've got this job in the supermarket. I had to
stay late.

WOMAN	You could have told me. I was actually beginning to worry.
PRECIOUS	I can look after myself.
WOMAN	That's not the point, Precious. What is it with you?
PRECIOUS	What do you mean?
WOMAN	You've got this attitude.
PRECIOUS	Yeah, yeah – heard it all before.
WOMAN	Listen to me!
PRECIOUS	You're acting like my mother.
WOMAN	And you're acting like someone who doesn't know they're born. We're not getting anywhere, are we?
PRECIOUS	What?
WOMAN	Perhaps we shouldn't meet any more.
PRECIOUS	Why do you say that?
WOMAN	You infuriate me, Precious.
PRECIOUS	I was just beginning to like you.
WOMAN	What?
PRECIOUS	You're alright.
WOMAN	I thought –
PRECIOUS	What?
WOMAN	You might think I'm a bit out of touch, past it.
PRECIOUS	You're alright.
WOMAN	You reckon? You've got a funny way of showing it.
PRECIOUS	It's hard sometimes, to show how you feel.
WOMAN	You look different today.
PRECIOUS	Do I?
WOMAN	You're in love.
PRECIOUS	Love? I wouldn't call it love.
WOMAN	I can see it in your eyes. It's changed you.
PRECIOUS	His name's Steve. He's nice. Are you OK?
WOMAN	I remember my first love.
PRECIOUS	Do you?
WOMAN	Twenty years ago now.
PRECIOUS	You loved him?

WOMAN   I think I did.

PRECIOUS   You seem sad today. Is something wrong? You usually wear a wedding ring.

WOMAN   I'm OK. Come on.

They approach a painting.

PRECIOUS   This is a wild sea, drawing me away, calling me, inviting...

WOMAN   I see the shape of a woman, in her arms a child. The child reaches out to her.

Another painting.

PRECIOUS   This one... is a beach on an island far away where the sun always shines and the sea laps the shore.

WOMAN   I see a desert – hills of deep, soft sand, impossible to climb. The sun is merciless. No escape.

Another painting.

PRECIOUS   The end of a long journey, light at the end of the tunnel – hope.

WOMAN   I see confusion, chaos, the hope of birth replaced by death. *(Precious continues to look at the paintings.)* He left today. Said we needed a break – think about what we really want from life and each other. I told him to go – go and find the mother of his children. It's not like that, he said. I feel like I've failed in some eternal way, let the whole world down. When I'm gone, who or what will I leave behind? What is my legacy? What evidence is there that I ever lived if not the love I give to a child? They tell me nobody's to blame. It's just nature's way and she never has to explain herself. Nothing I've done or not done – just left it too late. You can leave it too late. As simple as that. He says he loves me. I know I love him and we began with such hope. Will it all end in dust and ashes?

TOGETHER　It's an unbelievable feeling...
PRECIOUS　Of togetherness.
WOMAN　Of loneliness.
PRECIOUS　Someone –
WOMAN　No one –
TOGETHER　To talk to.
PRECIOUS　Someone –
WOMAN　No one –
TOGETHER　To hold, call my own.
PRECIOUS　Sometimes we sit and just look at each other and –
WOMAN　Time passes.
PRECIOUS　Flies past. He knows everything about me – and still likes me.
TOGETHER　I thought –
PRECIOUS　Nobody could want me.
WOMAN　That it must happen. Like it happens to everybody else.
TOGETHER　But I was wrong. I have never felt like this.

They exit.

7.
Kamala's bedroom. Kamala is tidying up and packing away clothes as Precious enters.

KAMALA　Precious!
PRECIOUS　Didn't you hear me knocking?
KAMALA　I said we can't meet today.
PRECIOUS　I know. I'm sorry. I was passing and saw your window open and – we haven't seen each other for ages.
KAMALA　Who's fault is that?
PRECIOUS　Mine. I know. Steve and I –
KAMALA *(pulls a face, mocking.)* Steve...

PRECIOUS   Don't be like that. I need to talk to you. I've got some news, big news.

KAMALA   You want to tell me, not Steve? Am I back in fashion? Lucky me. I'm surprised Mum let you in.

PRECIOUS   Why?

KAMALA   I told her I don't want to be disturbed, not today.

PRECIOUS   What are you doing?

KAMALA   What does it look like?

PRECIOUS   Going on holiday?

KAMALA   Wish I was. You've got big news? Is it bigger than this? *(She holds out her left hand to reveal an engagement ring.)* Wedding's in six weeks.

PRECIOUS   In America?

KAMALA   Florida.

PRECIOUS   So this is it?

KAMALA   There's nothing I can do about it, Precious.

PRECIOUS   You don't sound very happy. If you don't like him...

KAMALA   He's OK.

PRECIOUS   You're going to marry him.

KAMALA   I know...

PRECIOUS   He should be more than OK.

KAMALA   So what do you suggest I do? Run away? Go around the world with you? *(Their eyes meet)* Where would we live? What would we do for money?

PRECIOUS   I don't know –

KAMALA   There's always an answer, isn't there, Precious? Where there's a will there's a way. Nothing's impossible.

PRECIOUS   Everything's possible...

KAMALA   But? What's wrong?

PRECIOUS   We can't run away, Kamala.

KAMALA   Why not?

PRECIOUS *(strokes her stomach)* Things have changed. I'm –

KAMALA   All talk.

PRECIOUS   No, I'm not.

KAMALA   You don't mean anything you say.
PRECIOUS   I thought you were OK with all this.
KAMALA   I was. I am.
PRECIOUS   So?
KAMALA   I'm engaged, Precious. In a few weeks' time, I'll be married. I just can't get my head round it.
PRECIOUS   Takes a while to sink in – things that will change your life forever. Kamala? *(Precious looks idly at Kamala's plane ticket on the other side of the room.)* What's this? *(Kamala looks up to see Precious with the ticket.)* This is for tomorrow.

Kamala rushes over and snatches it from her.

KAMALA   You shouldn't be looking at that.
PRECIOUS   You're leaving tomorrow?
KAMALA   It was the only flight I could get.
PRECIOUS   You were going without seeing me?
KAMALA   I didn't want any fuss.
PRECIOUS   So if I hadn't come today… how could you leave without saying goodbye?
KAMALA   I thought it would be difficult. You might… say things.
PRECIOUS   What things?
KAMALA   Things I can't afford to listen to at the moment. It's easier this way.
PRECIOUS   You didn't trust me.
KAMALA   It's not that.
PRECIOUS   Kamala…
KAMALA   Don't –
PRECIOUS   You're my best friend.
KAMALA   Stop it! Stop it! I don't want to say goodbye. To this house, to my parents, even this town. And I certainly don't want to say goodbye to you. This is home. It's only now that I realise.
PRECIOUS   Oh Kamala! *(She hugs her.)* This place won't be the same without you.

KAMALA   You'll come and visit me, won't you? On your great adventure?

PRECIOUS   Try and stop me.

KAMALA   And we'll keep in touch.

PRECIOUS   Of course we will. Who else have I got to talk to?

KAMALA *(Beat)* What were you going to say?

PRECIOUS   When?

KAMALA   You started to say something earlier.

PRECIOUS   You've got enough on your mind. Come on. I'll give you a hand.

She helps Kamala to pack.
Lights fade.

8.
Precious and Woman sit side by side on a park bench.

WOMAN   So how do you feel?

PRECIOUS   Scared. Trapped.

WOMAN   What did your parents say?

PRECIOUS   They don't know.

WOMAN   You should tell them.

PRECIOUS   I can't. I just can't.

WOMAN   What about Steve?

PRECIOUS   Nobody knows except you. And that's how I want it to stay – for the time being anyway. What a stupid mess.

WOMAN   You have to tell someone, Precious.

PRECIOUS   I was going to tell Kamala but she's got enough on her mind.

WOMAN   You can't face this on your own.

PRECIOUS   I know. When I see someone my age pushing a pram, I think – you mug. That will never happen to me.

WOMAN   Life surprises us sometimes.

PRECIOUS   It was a surprise, alright.

WOMAN   Just takes getting used to. Give it time. It's not the worst thing that could happen.

PRECIOUS   Yes it is. It is for me. This is a disaster.

WOMAN   It's not a disaster.

PRECIOUS   It's the end.

WOMAN   The end of what?

PRECIOUS   The end of the life I wanted.

WOMAN   You just have to make adjustments – big adjustments. It's not impossible.

PRECIOUS   But very difficult.

WOMAN   Not impossible.

PRECIOUS   How will I cope?

WOMAN   Tell your parents.

PRECIOUS   No way.

WOMAN   They'll shout and scream for a few days but once they get over the shock, they'll support you.

PRECIOUS   You reckon?

WOMAN   I know they will. It's what parents do.

PRECIOUS   There's no room at home for me and a baby. Even I can see that. I'd have to go, find somewhere else to live. How could I have been so stupid?

WOMAN   You'll manage, Precious.

PRECIOUS   Will I?

WOMAN   Yes. And it will be worth it. When the baby comes, you'll love it more than anything.

PRECIOUS   I can just imagine what everyone will say: 'You could see it coming. What else would you expect from someone like her.'

WOMAN   Who cares what people think?

PRECIOUS   They'll never believe it was an accident, that I wanted something else for my life, something different, something I feel I was born to do. I'll be fulfilling their prophecy.

WOMAN   You can't let that thought rule your life.

PRECIOUS   But I want to fulfil my own prophecies. I want to say what will happen to me. I want to create my own future.

WOMAN   It isn't always the life we expect, Precious. But it will be a good life. A very good life.

9.

Kamala arrives in a strange place, puts down her suitcase and starts to unpack. Precious takes out her suitcase and starts to pack her clothes.

KAMALA   Dear Precious...

PRECIOUS   Dear Kamala... Hope you –

KAMALA   Arrived safely in Miami.

PRECIOUS   Bet the weather is –

KAMALA   Very warm. I'm not really used to it. But I'll survive.

PRECIOUS   The weather here is cold. Colder than usual.

KAMALA   Mum says you've had snow.

PRECIOUS   Don't expect you'll ever get snow out there.

KAMALA   Anil's parents met me at the airport. They seem nice. They have a beautiful house – not short of a bob or two. When I said this to them, they said, 'Who's Bob?'

PRECIOUS   I imagine everything seems strange to you.

KAMALA   It won't feel like home for a while. What do you get up to now I'm not there?

PRECIOUS   I've been doing more days at the supermarket. The more money I can save, the quicker I can get on with my life. There's this art course I want to do and I'm going to use the money to buy my materials. You'd be so proud of me – I've got a plan for my life, a vision. And I'm going for it. It's going to be really difficult, but I've made my decision.

KAMALA   I'm glad you know what you want now. This course sounds just right for you.

PRECIOUS   Dad says it's good therapy – get it all out of my system and prepare me for when I get a proper job. Mum and Dad have been brilliant, actually. Parents –

KAMALA   You only realise what they've done for you when it's too late and you're never too old to miss them.

PRECIOUS	I'm sorry I can't make it to your wedding.
KAMALA	I'm sorry you won't be there.
PRECIOUS	I'm sure it will all go well.
KAMALA	Without a hitch – if you see what I mean.
PRECIOUS	And to think –
KAMALA	Just a year ago...
PRECIOUS	We were walking to school together.
KAMALA	Dressed in uniform.
PRECIOUS	Wishing for a time when exams were over.
KAMALA	And we could be free.

Pause. Precious finishes her packing. Kamala stops to rest. Both appear anxious.

PRECIOUS	Take care, Kamala.
KAMALA	Good luck, Precious.
TOGETHER	Keep in touch.

Precious picks up her suitcase and sings her song. Exit Precious.

10.
Precious' bedroom. She is writing a letter.

PRECIOUS   Dear Steve... Thanks for your card. It was waiting for me when I arrived home from hospital. It must have been hard to know what to send. As far as I know, nobody makes cards that say, 'Sorry you had an abortion'. Mum and Dad came to pick me up. There was silence in the car on the way home. What was there to say? I feel empty now. Cold and empty. But at the same time, I feel like I've been given a second chance. I've signed up for an access course at college and I'm really looking forward to it. Out of all this, I suddenly realise what I *do* want from life – and I'm going for it. I couldn't have kept the baby, Steve. I hope you realise that now. It's all very well working out how you would have supported us and how you would have stood by me – and

how much you love me... it's all very well... I just hope that in
time, you can forgive and forget. I did the sensible thing.

She folds the letter and puts it in an envelope.
Lights fade.

11.
Precious is painting a mural. She wears overalls and her paints are
in tubes and pots rather than cans. Woman enters carrying a large
box.

PRECIOUS   Hi. *(Woman appears not to hear her.)* Haven't seen
   you for a while.
WOMAN   I heard.
PRECIOUS   Oh, right.

Woman crosses to the middle of the floor and kneels down, placing
the box beside her.

PRECIOUS   My first commission, kind of. The youth club knew I
   was doing this art course and –

Woman takes the lid off the box. Precious realises she is not listening
but persists.

PRECIOUS *(referring to her painting)* What's your expert opinion?
   Too much red?

Woman carefully lays out baby clothes on the floor in front of her.

WOMAN   I bought these a while ago. Seems a shame to throw
   them away. But I don't know what else to do with them.
   (Precious turns back to her painting.) What made you decide to
   get rid of your baby, Precious? Why did you decide to do that?
   Tell me.

PRECIOUS   I don't have to answer to you.

WOMAN   I will never have children of my own.

PRECIOUS   I'm sorry.

WOMAN   I've been trying to understand –

PRECIOUS   Our circumstances are completely different.

WOMAN   A baby is a baby. What about Steve?

PRECIOUS   What about him?

WOMAN   He would have stood by you.

PRECIOUS   That's what he said. Didn't get a chance to test him on it.

WOMAN   He offered you everything you need.

PRECIOUS   And nothing I want.

WOMAN   You split up?

PRECIOUS *(nods)* I'm not proud of this, you know.

WOMAN   But you're happy.

PRECIOUS   I'm free.

WOMAN   Look what it's cost you.

PRECIOUS   It wasn't an easy decision. I liked being pregnant. It sounds silly but I felt I belonged – to my baby, to other women. I was part of something. I felt special from the moment I knew. And there was a time when I thought, 'Yes, I can do this.'

WOMAN   So what changed your mind?

PRECIOUS   I just couldn't see how it was going to work. A baby just doesn't fit in to what I want for my life. And I couldn't do it to Steve – tie him down like that.

WOMAN   Steve didn't come into it.

PRECIOUS   Yes, he did.

WOMAN   The only person you were thinking of, was yourself. It's all about you, Precious.

PRECIOUS   No.

WOMAN   You're selfish.

PRECIOUS   I'm going for what I want in life.

WOMAN   You're seventeen, you don't know what you want.

PRECIOUS   Yes, I do.

WOMAN   You've got no perspective on your life. You've
made this huge decision –
PRECIOUS   It was my decision to make.
WOMAN   And you didn't know how to make a better one.
PRECIOUS   It was the sensible thing to do. It wasn't even a
proper baby – just a collection of cells and fluid –
WOMAN   It was a baby. It was a baby.

Precious is clearly shaken.

WOMAN   What if you knew, you would never get another
chance to have your own child. Would you do it, Precious?
Would you make the same choice? Would you?
(Precious starts to sing her song. Woman joins in.)
I want to push the sun back in the sky, tear down the moon at
night, roll everything back to the point when I was you.
PRECIOUS   And I will be you in years to come. Only time
separates us. Twenty years.
WOMAN   Twenty years that seem like nothing now as I stand
here confronted with you – the person I once was.
PRECIOUS   As I scrubbed at graffiti, I imagined myself back in
this town in the future, an artist in my own right. In the gallery, I
imagined my pictures hanging on the wall. I imagined myself
living the life I want. I conjured you up, dreamt you into life
because I couldn't see anyone I wanted to be. You inspired me
and when I hold my vision of you in my mind, I am stronger. I
can do anything. What do you want, Precious?
WOMAN   I want you to realise what you've done. I want the
turmoil in my head to stop.
PRECIOUS   I will always remember what I did. Always. It's the
only decision I can make now, the only way to fulfil my own
prophecy.
WOMAN   I had a choice.
PRECIOUS   And I'll never know if I was right or wrong.
WOMAN   But I remember now what it was like to be –
TOGETHER   Seventeen with my whole life ahead of me.

WOMAN *(to herself)* I remember you, Precious. I remember you
with your dreams and your energy and your passions and your
drive and your ambition. Nothing was going to stop you –
nothing. I can't turn back the clock but I can remember who I was
then. *(looks at Precious)* So I understand. And as understanding
comes, so does peace. Thank you, Precious.

PRECIOUS   Thank you, Precious.

*Precious and Woman sing Precious' song. Together, they fold the
clothes and put them back in the box. Their movements mirror each
other – they are one and the same person. Woman hands the box to
Precious. Precious exits. Woman goes over to the wall, picks up a
brush and finishes the mural. She signs it: 'POW'.*

12.

*A graveyard. Woman (i.e. older Precious) enters holding flowers and
kneels at a grave.*

WOMAN / PRECIOUS I still haven't got a proper job, Dad,
but I'm doing OK. My exhibition's on in town. I think you'd be
proud. I had some news recently. Not very good news. But it
made me understand more about life and about you. I know now
why you called me Precious. It was because you loved me. You
treasured me – your very own daughter, flesh and blood. You
gave me that name so I would always remember that no matter
who I was in the past or what I am now, no matter where I was
born or where I end up, even in a world of white-washed walls,
you wanted me to know that I am Precious.

She lays the flowers and exits.
Lights fade.

13.

*Outside a party. Music booms from inside. Kamala enters reading
'The Echo'.*

KAMALA   Dear Sir... I would like to comment on the graffiti that has remained on my property for twenty years. It was painted by a local artist at the outset of her career and is now of considerable artistic significance. Anyone who wishes, may view my boundary wall at number nine, The Birches. Many have commented on how fortunate I am to be the owner of such a magnificent work of art.

Kamala smiles to herself. Woman enters, coming out of the party.

WOMAN (PRECIOUS) Kamala!

KAMALA   Precious! *(They hug.)*

WOMAN (PRECIOUS) How are you?

KAMALA   How are you?

WOMAN (PRECIOUS) You look great.

KAMALA   So do you.

WOMAN (PRECIOUS) Didn't pick up the accent then?

KAMALA   No way. Still dropping my 'h's.

WOMAN (PRECIOUS) We weren't very good at keeping in touch.

KAMALA   Guilty.

WOMAN (PRECIOUS) Me too.

KAMALA   Can you believe it?

WOMAN (PRECIOUS) Twenty years. I don't recognise half the people here.

KAMALA   I thought it was just me. Couldn't resist a reunion, though – and when I heard you were coming –

WOMAN (PRECIOUS) You just had to turn up.

KAMALA   Of course.

WOMAN (PRECIOUS) It all worked out for you, then?

KAMALA   I suppose. We celebrated our anniversary last month. The kids planned a huge surprise party. How they managed to keep it from us, I shall never know. How about you? Mum said you got married.

WOMAN (PRECIOUS) Yes – we've been through a tough time recently but we're sorting things out.

KAMALA   Good. So did you ever make it round the world?

WOMAN (PRECIOUS) I've travelled a bit.

KAMALA   But ended up back here.

WOMAN (PRECIOUS) Not quite – a good few miles away. But this isn't a bad place.

KAMALA   It's alright. And the tagging – all makes sense now. I went to your exhibition today. I felt quite envious.

WOMAN (PRECIOUS) Really?

KAMALA   You've really made a name for yourself, given something to the world.

WOMAN (PRECIOUS) My legacy.

KAMALA   Yeah. *(Beat)* You seem happy, Precious,

WOMAN (PRECIOUS) You know what, Kamala – I think I am.

KAMALA   Where has the time gone, eh?

WOMAN (PRECIOUS) One minute we're girls, next we're grown women racing through middle age.

KAMALA   But still feeling like girls.

WOMAN (PRECIOUS) Yeah. Still feeling like girls.

The modern bhangra hit plays again. They put down their drinks and dance together.
Lights fade

The end.

Angela Turvey

Angela was born in East London and grew up in Hornchurch, Essex. She studied German at University and worked for *Lufthansa* before embarking on her career as a writer. Her play *A Fine Example* toured with Theatre Centre in 1995. She has written several plays for radio including *Barrel Boy*, which won a RIMA Award (2002) and *The Moon is Mine* (both BBC Radio 4). Work for television includes *Eastenders* and *Doctors*. She has created and co-created drama series for Scottish Media Group and Grundy International. She is currently working on commissioned projects in radio, theatre and television.

Look At Me

Look At Me

I was desperate to write about my own school years – at thirteen, I'd bunked off school for three years because I was bullied. I kind of assumed I'd sit at home and just write my demons out, so the process of research and development was a revelation.

Theatre Centre and the Mercury Theatre, found a group of disenchanted young people, collected from Pupil Referral Units around Essex. There were about a dozen of them aged between twelve and sixteen – difficult, noisy, rowdy, abrasive, funny, incredibly sensitive and smart as whips. Putting them all together in one room with us – writer, director, composer, other artists, teachers, was... interesting. Windows were smashed. The bar was broken into. Tempers ran high. One girl locked herself into the toilets, little gangs formed. Slowly, over the week, we all began to work as a team. They became more and more involved in the making of the play, from the music they wanted to make, to precisely setting down their speech as dialogue.

I went away feeling like I'd been to a mental spa. I threw away my previous ideas and started again from scratch, sobered by their critical judgement and having a new understanding of what they faced in their daily lives. When I had a first draft, we shared it with them. They liked some things passionately, hated others. They were already starting to change from the young people we'd spent an intense week with – they didn't let me get away with a wrong word or gesture. Their confidence had grown. Some had inevitably disappeared during the process, but some of those came back. One young woman had started re-attending school because she wanted to do Drama GCSE.

The play toured to schools and other venues and raised questions wherever it went. A year later, Theatre Centre took it on a nationwide tour of schools and other venues. I saw one show in a theatre, full of fourteen and fifteen year olds, where they interacted, throwing lines in, answering rhetorical questions, making comments – it was the best show I saw. The actors responded with joy and fire.

It's affected me hugely as a writer. I now miss the opportunity to work with my target audience before and during the writing of a play. So I'm now firmly hooked – best job of my working life.

Anna Reynolds

Look At Me

Anna Reynolds

First performed at the Mercury Studio, Colchester, 28th October, 1999, produced by the Mercury Theatre Company in association with Theatre Centre. Directed by Adrian Stokes, designed by Clare Birks. Lighting designed by Neville Milsom. Company Stage Manager – Elb Hall. Composer – Matthew Bugg.

STACEY	Rebecca Smart
JOHN	Tony Casement
MOOSE	Tim Treslove
KANDI	Nina Bhirangi
NICK	Tony Casement
HEADTEACHER /LAURIE	Tim Treslove
COUNSELLOR	Rebecca Smart

A second co-production by Theatre Centre and the Mercury Theatre, was first performed at Swanlea School, E1 in September 2000 with the following cast and creative personnel: Tina Gambe (Stacey), Richard Mansfield (John / Nick), Stuart Mullen (Moose / Head teacher), Lorraine Stanley (Kandi); Company Stage Manager – Marijke Zwart; ASM (Rehearsals) – Jenny Adshead; Co-Directors – Rosamunde Hutt / Adrian Stokes; Designer – Denise Amy-Rose Forbes; Composer – Matthew Bugg; Movement Director – Liam Steel; Voice Consultant – Bernadette O'Brien; Production Manager – Jane Mackintosh; Education Resources – Brenda Murphy; Graphic Design – Philip Bray; Production Photography – Hugo Glendinning.

With thanks to: Adrian Berry and staff at the Old Bull Arts Centre, Barnet; Alastair, the staff and students at the Pavilions Study Centre, Barnet; Curtis James; Dee Evans, Philip Bray and colleagues and all the artists and students who contributed to the research, development and initial production at the Mercury Theatre, Colchester.

1. Flashback (Fantasy)

Stacey and John are circling each other.

STACEY	Come on then.
JOHN	Alright.
STACEY	Yeh?
JOHN	Yeh. *(Stacey slaps him hard.)* What was that for?
STACEY	That was for you.

John slaps Stacey hard.

JOHN   And that was for you. *(Stacey walks away.)*
    That's it?
STACEY   Yeh. I'm bored.
JOHN   Right. Well, then, I'll see you. *(Stacey walks back
    and kicks him hard in the groin.)* Ooof! *(He collapses onto the
    floor. She pulls his head back by the hair, pleased.)* Ow.
STACEY   Now that hurts him. Say it.
JOHN   OW.
STACEY   *Really* hurts him. Say it.

Pause.

JOHN   Sorry.
STACEY   Too late.

Stacey slams his head against the floor. Music.

2. Present Time

STACEY   It's funny being back at school. You probably think I'm
    mad coming back here when I hated every minute of it. But all
    the years I've been away, every now and then I'll remember a
    corridor, or a classroom, and I'll stop dead in the middle of

whatever I'm doing. Like I'd left something here and now I've come back to find it. Only it feels like I never left at all. This is how it really happened.

3. Flashback (Reality)
Stacey and John circling each other.

STACEY   Come on then.

JOHN   Alright, let's just calm down-

STACEY   Why?

JOHN   Come back to class, Stacey.

STACEY   No.

JOHN   I really don't want to give you detention.

STACEY   Do it. I don't fancy going home anyway.

JOHN   Why not?

STACEY   I don't know. Why wouldn't I want to go home? You tell me, you're sleeping with my mother.

JOHN   I'm not sleeping with her, Stacey. I'm having a relationship with her.

STACEY   What's the difference?

JOHN   I'm not going to talk about it out here.

STACEY   You worried someone'll hear? The whole school knows you're giving my Mum one! It's doin my head in... *(He looks at his watch discreetly but she sees.)* My Dad would've hated you. When he comes back you'll be dead, I'm tellin you. Cause he is coming back.

JOHN   Come on, let's go.

STACEY   Make me. Go on. Take my arm and drag me back   in there, big hard man, go on show me what you're made of.

JOHN   Oh, don't tempt me. *(She teases him with a stage slap very near his face. He doesn't respond.)* Whatever's bothering you, we can talk about it later...

STACEY   No. Now.

JOHN   There's thirty kids in there waiting for you to make your mind up so I can get on with the lesson.

(She shrugs) If you get a third detention I'll have to inform your mother.

STACEY   That what you've been doing, Sir? *Informing* my mother? I never heard it called that before.

JOHN   Well? Up to you.

STACEY   Whatever.

She walks off dismissively.

JOHN   Yeh... Whatever.

He goes.

4. Present Time

Kandi comes on, sits down, perfectly composed. She's wearing a Walkman. Moose comes on, wearing a bomber jacket. He bends over Kandi, gesturing to her Walkman.

MOOSE   Take them off.

Kandi ignores him. Moose takes the headphones out of her ears.

KANDI   Do that for?

MOOSE   Pack it in and settle down.

Moose sits, clearly bored.

KANDI   Why ain't I got a teacher in here?

MOOSE   Short staffed. Think I wanna be here?

KANDI   Oh yeh and I do? I'm well bored man.

MOOSE   You ain't got time to be bored. You got lines
to do.

KANDI   No one does lines any more.

MOOSE   Whatever.

He sits back, folds his arms, closes his eyes, relaxes.

KANDI   You asleep?
MOOSE   Just resting me eyes.

She watches him. He's asleep. She flicks a bit of paper at him. No response.

KANDI   I could do anything I wanted right now. He's
well asleep, in he? I could.. take all my clothes off. Run away. Set
him on fire.

She flicks her lighter dangerously close to him several times. No response.

KANDI   I could do anything.

She puts her lighter away.

KANDI   But I don't want to. Sad.

Stacey comes in. Kandi puts her head down and starts writing. Stacey looks at what Kandi's writing.

STACEY   Dear Mr Simmons, I'm sorry I said that you had –
wow. That's not a disease I've even heard of.

Stacey sits on Moose's lap as if he were a chair. He doesn't stir. Kandi stares.

KANDI   You an inspector, Miss?
STACEY   How many lines, Kandi?
KANDI   I gotta say why I'm sorry in five hundred words.
STACEY   Are you sorry?

KANDI *(shrugs)* I know I was out of order.

STACEY Yeh? Good for you. I never did. Don't you mind being on your own in here?

KANDI Better than being in class.

STACEY Why's that?

KANDI *(shrugs, suddenly closed)* Dunno, Miss. Just is.
(She starts writing again. Stacey gets off Moose. She goes behind Kandi, takes her pen and starts writing. The handwriting is exactly the same, but very fast.)
That's wicked, Miss, can you do cheques?
(Stacey laughs. She and Kandi make eye contact. Stacey leaves. Kandi puts her headphones back in. Moose wakes up instantly. He motions to her, take it off. She does. She writes in silence.)
You was well asleep, you pig.

MOOSE I was not.

KANDI An inspector come in. She saw you.

MOOSE *(sits up, slightly worried)* You're having a laugh.

KANDI You was so asleep she sat on your lap.

MOOSE Liar.

KANDI Write out fifty times: I Must Not Call Students Names. Er – if you can write, that is...

There's an awkward silence. He can't.

MOOSE If someone come in here – you better speak up now, girl.

Kandi ignores him. She writes slowly, taunting, sings under her breath.

KANDI You're on the door at *Hollywood's*, aren't you?

MOOSE No. I'm stuck in a classroom with a retard.

KANDI Yeh, that's funny – you can't write and I'm the retard? You wanna explain that to the Head?

MOOSE Sorry.

KANDI   Sorry just ain't good enough. You are well out of order. I could have you sacked for that.

MOOSE   Alright! Alright... What d'you want?

KANDI   I *want* to get in the club as soon as I turn up. I *don't* want – a queue, hassle about how I'm dressed, anyone touching me up, being charged to get in. Some respect. That's what I want. Alright? *(He doesn't look at her.)* Alright?

Moose looks at her. She smiles.

5. Flashback.
Stacey's alone. Moose comes on and sits down.

MOOSE   We had a laugh last night, innit?

STACEY   Oh yeh. Watching you neck twelve pints is well funny, Moose.

MOOSE   Come here.

STACEY   Why?

MOOSE   I like the way your fat bum moves.

STACEY   Take that back or I'm leavin you.

MOOSE   I love your fat bum. Come here, Peaches.

STACEY   Don't call me Peaches.

MOOSE   Don't call me Moose.

STACEY   Will if I want.

MOOSE   You can do anything you like, darlin. I'm putty in your tiny little hands.

Stacey freezes him.

6. Present Time.

STACEY   Stay. Good boy. You'd never believe he used to spend his spare time robbing off-licences and hitting policemen. I s'pose that's why I liked him at first, because he was the opposite of everything right. But that didn't mean he was wrong. If I'd

been able to love him, who knows whatd've happened? The past
is putting its claws in me again.

*Stacey sends Moose off. She goes. Kandi and Nick come on. They sit
down and start writing. Kandi casts curious glances at Nick.*

KANDI   What you in here for? *(Nick gives her a look.)*
What you done? *(He ignores her.)* Must have done something to
be in here. Been a bad boy?

NICK   Shut up or they'll send somebody in, alright?

KANDI   They ain't got enough teachers today. I heard
them sayin. What you done? *(He does not respond)*
I was well rude right? You listening to me? I told the teacher to
go do himself up the arse. He didn't say anything for ages, it was
weird, everyone was looking at me? And his eyes were all filling
up like he was gonna cry or something... I don't even know why I
done it. Funny innit? *(He does not respond)*
Why don't nobody listen to me?

NICK   It ain't my fault.

KANDI   It's nobody's fault. You could listen to me. I mean
it's only you and me in here..

NICK   I just wanna finish this and go home so do one.

KANDI   Oh boring, boring. I want to go out. I want to live. I
don't want to be here with you.

NICK   Nobody wants to be.*(puts his head down and writes)*

KANDI   I wish I could just shut up sometimes but... I can't.
What's your name?

NICK   Nick.

KANDI   Listen, Nick, this ain't really me. I'm really quiet in
class, you ask anyone, but just once in a while I can't stand it –

NICK   Shut up! You're ruining it for me.

KANDI   It's like my face is nearly cracking, I'm trying so
hard to smile just like everyone else. Why won't anybody
LISTEN TO ME?

Stacey comes in. Kandi sees her. Nick doesn't.

KANDI	I'm not like this all the time – she heard me!
NICK	Who –?
KANDI	What you talkin about? She's like an inspector or

something –

NICK	You're weird.
KANDI	She's right here, in front of you – you blind or – or –

Stacey smiles at her. Kandi understands.

NICK	Or your pathetic imagination.
KANDI	Yeh.

Stacey freezes Nick. Kandi is frightened.

STACEY	OK, Kandi. I'm listening.
KANDI	Uh?
STACEY	You wanted somebody to listen to you.
KANDI	Can he hear me? *(Stacey shakes her head.)*

Can he hear you? *(Beat)* No, he can't, can he? He can't hear you
and he can't see you. Why not? How come I can? Am I going
mad? No. I'm dreaming. Always dreaming, that's why I end up in
here, that and me big gob. I fell asleep in class once and nobody
noticed, till the teacher put his clammy hand on me. Then I
shouted at him for touching me. Got three days for that.

STACEY	Why were you asleep?
KANDI	Dunno.
STACEY	Don't waste my time.
KANDI	S'pose I was tired.
STACEY	Why were you tired?
KANDI	If this is still a dream I can say.
STACEY	You'd like it to be a dream?
KANDI	I like dreams where you're safe... Who are you?
STACEY	It's your dream. You choose.

KANDI   You're my... mother. No. Sister... maybe. No – I dunno. You're a total stranger. Like someone you meet on a bus or when you're pissed and you just tell them things. You know?

STACEY   I know.

KANDI   Yeh. Cause... cause you have to say things, sometimes, or it's like you'll explode and all this *stuff'll* just come out like poison, no warning, just all the badness inside me coming out for everyone to see. *(Pause.)*
I was tired cos I couldn't sleep.
I couldn't sleep cos I wasn't in bed.
I wasn't in bed cos I was out.
I was out cos I was shagging someone.
Well, they were shagging me really.
Yeh. I think it went like that. Pocket money.
You still listening stranger?

STACEY   Oh yes.

KANDI   When's that bloody bus coming then?

STACEY   Depends where you want to go.

KANDI   Somewhere... nice.

STACEY   Somebody once said to me; if you always face forward, everything bad will be behind you.

KANDI   That's cool...
(They exchange tentative smiles. Stacey goes.)
Don't go. I might wanna say something else –

STACEY   Later.

KANDI   Promise?

7. Rewind.

Nick starts writing. Kandi stares at him. Stacey goes.

KANDI   What you doing? *(He ignores her.)*
What you done? Must have done something to be in here... Been a bad boy?

NICK   Shut up or they'll send somebody in alright?

KANDI   No, go on, tell me? I'm listening.

NICK	Leave it, OK?
KANDI	OK.

They both start writing. They peek at each other.

NICK	I'm Nick.
KANDI	I know.
NICK	How d'you know?
KANDI	Uh... I heard some boy call your name.
NICK	Yeh? I've only been here a week.
KANDI	Yeh, well, a week's a long time innit? I'm Kandi. With a K?
NICK	Yeh? Nice to meet you, Kandi with a K.

Nick holds his hand out. Kandi gives him one of her headphones to listen to. Music. Moose comes in.

MOOSE	Oi! I've told you –
KANDI	Oh, *man,* what is it with you?

Moose tries to take the Walkman off her. Kandi pushes him away, aggressively. The Walkman falls and breaks.

8. Flashback.

JOHN	Again.
STACEY	I've told you.

John waits. Stacey sighs.

STACEY	Mrs G asks me to get the video out of the video cupboard, right?
JOHN	Right.

STACEY   But the lead gets caught on something, I can't see
what, and I'm pulling away at it, right, and she's shouting down
the corridor, what's taking so long Stacey? and I'm getting really
flustered because she thinks I'm stupid, she's always getting at
me for not doing things right, being slow and that. So she comes
down the corridor after me, I can hear those squeaky shoes
getting nearer, and she's behind me, I can smell her sweaty-

JOHN   Don't embroider –

STACEY   – so I say, the lead's caught, miss, it's not my fault,
I'm trying, and she pushes me out of the way/ and –

JOHN   /Roughly?

STACEY   What? No, not really, just – and then she gives it a
tug and the leads flies out. So simple. And she says, *can't you get
anything right?* And then somehow I'm closing the door on her
and before I know it I'm standing outside the cupboard, with the
keys swinging from my hand.

JOHN   And how big is the cupboard, Stacey? (*Stacey
frames a vague, small shape with her hands.*) Small.

STACEY   Smallish. But then she is small herself, innit, and
matter is all relative... I done that in science.

JOHN   She's probably terrified in there.

STACEY   I don't think she's frightened of anything, Sir.
Anyhow she's probably clawed her way out by now.
(*He makes a clawing gesture.*) You hate her as much as I do. Let
her sweat.

JOHN   Alright, that's enough. Give me the keys.

Stacey shakes the keys at him.

JOHN   Don't be bloody stupid.

STACEY   Ooh, you swore.

JOHN   You trying to get yourself thrown out?

STACEY   I don't really care, Sir.

JOHN   Because if you were smart, you'd make a complaint
about Mrs G. About the way she talked to you, things she's said.
You wouldn't be the first, but you didn't hear that from me.

STACEY   Yeh, right. Who'd believe me?

JOHN   I would. Everyone. Your Mum would.

STACEY   I don't think my Mum's any of your business any more, sir. You're past history, long gone.

JOHN   Yeh, you did a great job there, Stacey. Happy now?

STACEY   Ecstatic, Sir. *(She teases him with the keys. He catches her arm.)* Get off me. You're hurtin!

JOHN   Give me the keys then.

STACEY   She's seeing this other bloke anyway –

JOHN   Let go of the keys.

STACEY   Let go of me or I'll scream the place down and you know I can. *(He grabs the keys and lets go of her.)* You are so sweaty. If the head saw you now...

JOHN   Yeh, you'd like to see me out of a job? *(She shrugs.)* You know what I'd like? I'd like you to surprise me. *(He puts the keys in his desk drawer.)*

STACEY   What you doing?

JOHN   In one minute one of us is going to unlock that cupboard and let Mrs G out.

STACEY   So? It ain't gonna be me.

JOHN   Just for once, Stacey, prove everybody wrong.

Stacey freezes John.

STACEY   Alright. What d'you think he's playin at? He don't care about Mrs G any more than I do but... God, if only she could stay in there for a little bit longer. Like a week? He's sayin, let her out now and you're safe. Or he unlocks her and she comes out of there like a bull and it's over, I'm out, bye bye Stacey, have a nice life on the rubbish heap. Just cause I don't wanna do this simple thing. *(She pauses, like she's listening to someone.)* You think I should let her out? I CAN'T HEAR YOU. Let her out? No. But, 'Surprise me', he says. 'Prove me wrong.' I hate it when they say that.

Stacey unfreezes John and holds her hand out for the keys.

JOHN   Woah, hold on – Why the sudden change of heart?

STACEY   Dunno. Come on, before I bottle out.

JOHN *(gets the keys out, hesitates.)* What's your story?

STACEY   I got sick of being told I was nothing.

JOHN   And..?

STACEY   I flipped.

JOHN   Not much of a story is it?

STACEY   It's all there is... give us the keys. *(He gives her the keys. She lingers.)* You gonna back me up?

JOHN   What do you think?

STACEY   I mean, afterwards... When she bursts out...

JOHN   Trust me.

STACEY   Trust you. That's funny.

JOHN   Yeh.. Go on, get it done.

Stacey goes off. John follows her.

9. Present Time.

Kandi sits opposite the Headteacher, Laurie, in an office.

LAURIE   Do you know why you're in here?

A long, uncomfortable beat. Kandi tries to out-stare Laurie. Eventually she mumbles.

KANDI   I hit the caretaker, Sir.

LAURIE   Yes... Why did you hit him?

KANDI   Dunno, Sir.

LAURIE   You don't know?

KANDI   No. Sir.

LAURIE   Had he – provoked you in any way?

Pause. Stacey comes in and perches on Kandi's chair arm.

LAURIE   Had he done anything to –

KANDI   I know what provoked means, Sir.

LAURIE   Well, had he?

KANDI   He tried to take my Walkman off me, Sir.

LAURIE   Your Walkman that you shouldn't be wearing in school, anyway?

KANDI   No, the other one. Sir.

LAURIE   What other one?

STACEY   Oooh... Watch yourself here. Be careful.

KANDI   Nothing Sir.

LAURIE   You know the number one rule here, don't you Kandi?

KANDI   Yeh Sir.

LAURIE   What is it?

KANDI   No violence.

LAURIE   Yes. *(Pause)* The thing is, Kandi... the thing is, I know you're having some problems at home.

KANDI   I ain't got a home.

LAURIE   Well, OK, I know that's difficult, but I will not tolerate violence from anybody in my school. I'm going to have to exclude you. You do have the right to –

KANDI   Wait a minute – you're kicking me out for this?

LAURIE   You've given me no choice! If you can't control your behaviour I can't have you here. *(Pause)* You might be better off in a different school, perhaps a smaller –

KANDI   I don't wanna move. I know people here...

LAURIE   I understand that, but in a smaller school –

KANDI   I'm getting good marks!

LAURIE   I know. Which makes my job even harder, but there is a limit. I want to try and keep you here, but you're not helping me, are you? *(Stacey goes behind Laurie and leans on his chair.)*

STACEY   You can be dumb or you can be smart, Kandi. It's up to you. I mean, this guy just wants you OUT. Whatever he says.

KANDI   He is alright, in he, the caretaker? *(Stacey smiles.)*

LAURIE   Yes, but that's not the point. Next time –
KANDI   There won't be a next time!
LAURIE   You can promise me that, can you? *(Pause)*
You can't even keep your temper in check with me. I'm sorry,
Kandi, I won't put other people at risk until you can –
KANDI   So when can I come back?

*A long beat. Laurie looks away. A terrible silence. Before Kandi
takes it in. Stacey freezes Laurie.*

KANDI   Not a dream this time. Who *are* you?
STACEY   No time, love. Listen, the caretaker shouldn't have
even been in the room with you; it should have been a teacher. It
isn't his fault but use whatever you need. He tried it on with you?
Put his hand on your leg, tried –
KANDI   No! That's out of order.
STACEY   OK. Let's see. Your whole future is at stake. Your
family will be devastated.
KANDI   I ain't got a family.
STACEY   I told you – use whatever you need to, Kandi. This is
war. Are you up for this?
KANDI   Ye–eh.
STACEY   Are you sure?
KANDI   Yeh!
STACEY   OK. Let's try it again.

10. Rewind.

LAURIE   Had he provoked you in any way? *(Kandi looks
away, thinking, weighing it up)* Kandi?
STACEY   Trust me.
KANDI   I want my Mum.
LAURIE   I know the last year's been very hard for you.
KANDI   You don't know *nothing*, man.
STACEY   Let him help you.

KANDI   Sorry. I'm really sorry. It's just sometimes I can't –
LAURIE   Look –
KANDI   ...keep it in, you know? I get –
LAURIE   I know things're difficult but –
KANDI   I got nothing else now. I got nothing. I don't wanna
have to start again, Sir. I can't handle it...
LAURIE   Don't start crying. That's not going to help.

*Kandi is fighting tears. Stacey raises Kandi's face up; Laurie can see
how distressed she is. Kandi fights her; she's mortified at crying in
front of Laurie.*

STACEY   Good girl. You show him.
LAURIE   I'm excluding you for three days. There'll be an
appointment with a counsellor – I expect you to keep it. It might
help you to talk to someone.
KANDI   I don't need to talk.
STACEY   That's what I always said. It's a lie.
LAURIE   Kandi, this is a last chance. Do you understand how
serious this is now?

Kandi is silent.

STACEY   Yes, Sir.
KANDI   Yeh Sir.
LAURIE   Because there won't be a next time.
KANDI   I know.
LAURIE   That'll be it.
KANDI   Yeh.
LAURIE   Look... I'm really sorry about your Mum.
KANDI   My *mother*. Can I go now?
LAURIE   Yeh, go on. But remember what I said.

Kandi leaves. Laurie rubs his eyes wearily.

LAURIE   Why the hell did I do that? She'll be out within a month anyway, I'd put money on it.

STACEY   Don't be so sure, sir.

Laurie goes.

STACEY   Do you see why I'm here now? Why I've come back? I'm here to have fun. To cause trouble. To set the school cat among the playground pigeons. That's my story anyhow. This is how it goes: time's running out for Kandi. Nick too, he's had two detentions in a week. What's that I hear? Tick tock, tick tock, watch them run against the clock. My turn.

11. Flashback.
Stacey sits on the floor. John sits beside her.

JOHN   Wasn't so bad after all, was it?

STACEY   Mmm. You see her face when she fell out of the cupboard?

They both begin to laugh and quickly stop.

STACEY   Why d'you bother? I don't get it.

JOHN   Why do you think?

STACEY   Cause you wanna get back with my Mum?

JOHN   Maybe I don't want Mrs G to have the satisfaction of kicking you out.

Stacey puts a fiver on the floor.

STACEY   She'll have me out within a month. Bet me?

JOHN   No. You're smarter than that.

STACEY   She ain't gonna let this drop.

JOHN   That's up to you. You've only got another year and a half then you can leave anyway.

Stacey freezes John.

STACEY   *Only another year and a half?* I couldn't even imagine sticking it that long. I knew I'd win that bet because it was easier than staying. I had the feeling that if I had to stand another week of school I'd – not explode, exactly. I'd sort of melt down. I'd be sitting in class and Mrs G'd be saying, 'Romeo and Juliet, second act. When Romeo leaves, how does Juliet feel?' And I'd know exactly what she felt, I could have talked til the bell went, but I'd sit there with me hand up and she'd pick anyone else rather than me. She never even looked me in the face again and I knew she'd win in the end. Cause I didn't see the future coming til it hit me in the face. *(She lets John go.)* Listen – *(Pause. She is soo uncomfortable.)* No, forget it.

JOHN   What? Come on.

STACEY   My Mum, right...

JOHN   How is she?

STACEY   Yeh. She's – She needs something to take her mind off... me. She's not very happy. Are you?

JOHN   Are you?

STACEY   You first. *(Beat)*

JOHN   No.

The bell goes.

JOHN   Torture over. You can go. *(He gets up.)*

STACEY   She's in tonight. *(Pause)* All I'm saying is you could go round tonight. I won't be there.

JOHN   You won't be sweating over your homework in the living room?

STACEY   That's irony, right?

JOHN   Very good. You've been secretly paying attention in my lesson, yeh? *(He touches the fiver with his foot.)* You did surprise me.

STACEY   Yeh, well, it was a one-off.

JOHN   Doesn't have to be.

STACEY *(gets up)* Look, you gonna see her or not? *(He picks up
     her fiver and keeps it. He hands her a fiver from his pocket. She
     tucks it into her waist.)* She'd have you back if you ask nicely.

JOHN   Unfair. Insider information.

STACEY   No. I can see into the future.

JOHN   Sure you can.

He goes.

STACEY   Sure I can. I can see you walking into the staffroom,
     trying not to think about what I've said. If I was you, I'd be
     running along the road to my house before it's too late. Cause you
     don't always get second chances..

12. Present Time.
*Nick sits on the bench in the town centre. He's twitchy. Stacey
watches.*

NICK   She's late.

STACEY   She's not that late.

NICK   Dunno how long to wait…

STACEY   Thirty minutes I'd say.

NICK   Where is she?

*Stacey snaps her fingers. Kandi appears; dressed up in front of a
mirror. She looks wonderful. She checks out her arse. She sees
Stacey and jumps.*

KANDI   Don't do that! You're like always there.

STACEY   I can go in the blink of an eye.

KANDI   Yeh?

STACEY   Yeh. Snap your fingers and I'll be gone.

Kandi holds her fingers together. Nearly clicks, testing.

STACEY   –if you're sure you want me to go. *(Kandi turns back to the mirror.)* You're beautiful.

Kandi turns away.

KANDI   Bollocks am I.

STACEY   Yeh, you are. Don't make him wait too long.

KANDI   Why not?

STACEY   Just don't. You don't know anything about him.

KANDI   *You* don't know nothin/ about *me* –

STACEY   /I know all about you.

A long beat.

STACEY   Look at me.

KANDI   I'm looking.

STACEY   No. *Look at me.* Can anybody else see me?

KANDI   I dunno. These shoes alright?

STACEY   Listen. You've seen me now. You'll never forget me. You might think you will, but I'll come back to you, maybe in the dead of the night. When you're least expecting it. You'll never be able to say, *no one ever listened to me.* Remember that. The shoes are good.

KANDI   Yeh?

STACEY   Yeh.

KANDI   Is he still waiting for me?

STACEY   Course he is.

KANDI   I don't wanna go. I'll just make a fool of myself, open my big mouth and mess it all up. I'm not goin.

STACEY   OK. I'm wasting my time, then. I thought you had balls.

KANDI   Balls? No, I ain't got none of those man.

STACEY   I thought you had... something about you. I chose you, Kandi. And that makes you lucky. 'Cause some people never get chosen by anybody.

KANDI	Did you?
STACEY	Yeh. I just didn't know it at the time.

Kandi looks at herself again, unsure.

KANDI	What's your name?
STACEY	Stacey. *(Beat)* You can be whatever you want.
KANDI	Yeh, right.
STACEY	Trust me. I haven't let you down yet.

Stacey goes. Kandi looks at herself again, shy.

KANDI   'You're beautiful.' Bollocks.

13. *Nick and Kandi in* **Present Time.**
Moose and Stacey in **Past.**

MOOSE   She's late. And I won't have that.

NICK   She's forty minutes late in the end.

MOOSE   But then she's suddenly there, in front of me.

NICK   But then she's there, in front of me, and she's wearing this – this dress. Oh God. I want to turn around and go home and change or leave town or something I dunno, she just looks so –

MOOSE   She just looks so –

BOTH   Beautiful.

MOOSE   I mean I can't believe my luck.

NICK   I want to kiss her hands just because she's turned up at last, I mean how sad is that?

MOOSE   I always fancied her, but it's a joke innit? Stacey going out with the Moose, the lads would've ripped me to pieces for telling stories. But here she is! The Queen of the night! In a dress! And her hands are shaking, but I know better than to point that out.

NICK We were just walking round town all night, shivering. It's still warm out. I don't dare touch her in case I let her know how scared I am. Her eyes are lit up like fireworks. Is she on something? She could be anything. She could be anyone. I don't care. And when we're outside the place where she lives, which she says isn't home, she says it's *a* home, when we're there–

MOOSE Funny cause I'm always taking girls out. It ain't that big of a deal. I know what I'm doing, I know I'm heading for the good life, know what I'm saying? But Stacey... oh my God, Stacey don't play by the rules. Stacey don't even know the rules exist.

NICK I kiss her. Oh God I kiss Kandi with a K. It's funny. It's not as though she's never been kissed before. I've heard – things about her. About what she gets up to with boys. With men.

MOOSE Like I take her home. And we stand outside for a while, and I'm thinkin, about time to dive in, and she suddenly says, *take me home.* Now the thing is, she's already *at* home.

Stacey comes on.

STACEY I don't want to go in, because I can see John's in there. He's done what I told him. You're holding his hand, Mum, you're not crying but I can tell it's not far off. The last thing you want is me walking in. And you know the Moose is trouble, everyone knows that but he's all I've got suddenly and I know it won't cost me much to make him happy. That's how it starts.

MOOSE And then I know that she's mad for me. *Result.*

Kandi comes on, edgy, excited.

KANDI Nick.

NICK When I kiss her, it's like nobody's ever... I'm not even unhappy but when I touch Kandi, I feel... I feel amazing. I feel alive. I'm... don't tell anyone but I'm almost looking forward to going to school tomorrow because she'll be there. God I haven't done my homework. *(He goes off quickly.)*

KANDI   Nick.

STACEY   And I'm still there three weeks later, in his
maisonette, discovering how his mind works. And his washing
machine and where his fridge is, because you know what's weird?
They're all hidden behind doors, so nothing's what it seems.
Sometimes I call you, Mum, but you're so happy with the teacher
I don't even know what to say. You even ask me to come home
but let's face it, it's easier if I don't. And the funny thing is, I'm
still going to school. Just. For the Moose. It's the only thing he
ever asks me to do.

Stacey goes.

KANDI   Nick. I just wanna say his name as many times as I
can before I have to go back to the home.

MOOSE   I ain't kidding myself. I know why she's here, she
ain't got anywhere else to go. Some people might think I was
takin' advantage but who's usin who? She can't even find the
fridge but I love her and that's hard to say.

Moose goes.

KANDI   'Cause I don't know nobody here. I don't wanna
know nobody here because I ain't planning on staying that long. I
just wanna dance and dance, until my feet fall off. I just wanna
dance. I don't care what happens to me. *(Beat)* Stacey? Where are
you when I need you?

14. Present Time.
Kandi and Counsellor.

COUNSELLOR We'll probably meet once a week or so. Is that
OK?

KANDI   Whatever, Miss.

COUNSELLOR My name's Liz. Call me Liz. *(Kandi is silent.)*
So, Kandi, you've been having problems at school.

KANDI Have I?

COUNSELLOR Can you tell me why?

KANDI I think it could be cause school's shit, Miss.

COUNSELLOR Liz. OK, why do you think school's shit?

KANDI Because it is. Nobody ever listens – *(Beat)*

COUNSELLOR Nobody ever listens to you?

KANDI No, that ain't it. I wanna go home, Miss.

COUNSELLOR Where's home?

KANDI You've read my files in't you, why do I have to tell
you? My Mum's dead, my Dad can't handle it, Fi and Tone have
gone to foster parents and I'm – d'you know what I mean, I'm
here, so...

A silence.

COUNSELLOR Are you missing your Dad?

KANDI Next question, Miss.

Counsellor is silent.

KANDI Ask me something.

COUNSELLOR Would you like to see him?

KANDI No.

COUNSELLOR Why not?

Kandi looks around for Stacey. She holds her fingers together.

COUNSELLOR What's the matter, Kandi?

KANDI Nothing, Miss.

A silence.

COUNSELLOR It seems as though you're angry about everything that's happened to you and perhaps you're taking that out on other people. Like teachers. Like me?

A silence. Kandi stands up, ready to go.

KANDI You think I couldn't work that out for myself? *(Counsellor is silent.)* Look, I just – want to go back to school. I just want my Mum, OK – *(She is nearly crying. Counsellor doesn't comfort her.)* – and she ain't here and she's never gonna be here again and I know that, I ain't stupid, so – so just fuck off, OK. There it goes again, my big mouth, that's my last five days isn't it?

COUNSELLOR I'm sorry?

KANDI You what?

COUNSELLOR I didn't hear you.

KANDI I said that's my last five days...

She gets it.

COUNSELLOR Let's just get a few things straight. I'm here to help you stay in school, right. That's the most important thing. I'm not your enemy, alright? So sit down. Please.

Kandi dithers then sits.

15. Present Time.
Nick and Moose in the detention room.

NICK Hangman?

MOOSE Go on then. What is it, a film or somethin'? *(Nick shakes his head.)* Give us a clue.

NICK No. Letter.

MOOSE F... *(Nick smiles and draws a scaffold stand.)* A... *(Nick puts A in the line.)* Score. Uh – B... *(Nick draws a scaffold line.)*

C... *(Nick draws a scaffold line.)*
D... *(Nick puts D into the word.)* Song? Book? *(Beat)* Don't you
ever speak?
NICK   Letter.
MOOSE   D... H..?

Nick draws a noose. He smiles at Moose.

NICK   Nearly dead.
MOOSE   You're a strange lad, eh?
NICK   Did she hurt you? *(fills in a K, an N and an I)*
MOOSE   Who?
NICK   Kandi with a K.
MOOSE   You're havin a laugh. So tell me what *you* done.
(Nick shrugs.) Still playin games, yeh? Alright. You hit someone.
(Nick draws a scaffold stand.) Swearin at a teacher? Spittin?
(Nick draws a scaffold line.) Bullying? *(Nick looks at him
pityingly. Draws a line.)* No, you ain't the type. Skipping school?
(Nick half draws a line.) Being bullied? *(Nick puts the pen down.)*
What for? I don't get it. You're a smart lad, you ain't bad lookin'
... You serious? *(Nick wipes the slate clean.)* So, what, you kick
off once in a while?
NICK   Yeh, why not?
MOOSE   You fight back?
NICK   Yeh, but it's four on one, it ain't fair!
MOOSE   Have you told the teachers? *(Nick stares at him.)*
Ain't you got any mates?
NICK   Only been here two weeks!
MOOSE   Don't know anyone?
NICK   Just... Kandi.
MOOSE   Oh. You, eh, doin' her?
NICK   No! I'm, seeing, have seen once, you know... we've
– I don't know what I'm doing.
MOOSE   Yeh. Nor me, mate. I ain't got a clue.

Nick sits down.

NICK   You got a girlfriend?

MOOSE   Ain't you got some work to do? *(He shows him a sheet of writing.)* Yeh, great.

NICK   You can read it, if you want.

MOOSE   No, you're alright.

NICK   I want /somebody to –

MOOSE   Look I /ain't a teacher.

NICK   ... see it before I /hand it in.

MOOSE   Listen /mate, I can't read, so leave it.

NICK   Oh. Right. Not at all?

MOOSE   Road signs.

NICK   Useful.

MOOSE   Can't drive, can I?

NICK   Didn't you go to school?

MOOSE   Once or twice. I've done alright, hasn't been a problem. I'm working, en' I? Got money in my pocket. You can say the same at my age, you're doin alright.

NICK   You got kids?

Stacey comes in. She watches him.

STACEY   You be careful what you say to him.

MOOSE   Yeh, I got a boy near your age.

STACEY   No, you don't.

NICK   Yeh? What's he called?

MOOSE   Called?

NICK   What's his name?

MOOSE   I don't know, mate.

NICK   You don't know his name?

MOOSE   He's adopted, in he?

NICK   Yeh? So's my Dad.

A long beat.

STACEY	Tommy. His name was Tommy.
NICK	D'you ever wonder what he's like?
MOOSE	No.
STACEY	Liar.
MOOSE	Not much. So, this –

Moose flicks the paper Nick's written.

MOOSE   You could always read it to me.

NICK   Read?

MOOSE   Yeh, why not? We got nothing better to do.

NICK   I can't read it out. Feel stupid.

MOOSE   Don't put yourself down, boy. You can do whatever
you want. I did.

STACEY   No, you didn't. Look at you.

NICK   You wouldn't understand it anyway, so what's the
point?

STACEY   He might.

MOOSE   I might. Just cause I can't read – I done alright. I
ain't nothing. You don't know... I could have been nothing so
easy without her and I ain't.

He looks away, embarrassed.

NICK   The, the question was; how does Juliet respond to
the events of this scene? Do you know *Romeo and Juliet?*
(Moose and Stacey laugh.)
If I – I kind of tell you, what happens in the play? Because then
what I've written – you might understand it better?
(Moose shrugs.) OK. Right. Uh – there's these two families,
yeh, and they're always fighting...

Stacey freezes Nick. She puts her arms round Moose.

16. Flashback.

STACEY   Say it.

MOOSE   I love you even though you're/ a bitch –

STACEY   /Not that, fool. The one I taught you. Say it.

MOOSE   Let me be taken, let me be put to death. I am content so thou wilt have it so. I have more care to stay than will to go... That one?

STACEY   That one. By now I'm three months pregnant. Moose doesn't have a clue. I go to school to sign in and throw up in their toilets. While I'm retching I read the graffiti. '*Stacey Tasker is a loser.*' Like I didn't know this. It could have said, Stacey Tasker is scared out of her mind. Or, Stacey Tasker's about to ruin her life. It could of said a lot of things. But it didn't.

Nick unfreezes.

NICK   And there's Romeo, right, who's like in love with Juliet? and their families –

MOOSE   Eh?

NICK   You listening?

MOOSE   I'm listening, boy.

NICK   Nick.

MOOSE   Nick. Don't ever fall in love, Nick. It breaks your heart.

17. Present Time.

STACEY   The day they kick me out I know what's coming because they ask me to bring my Mum. You never say a word on the bus but I can feel you want to. In the Headmaster's office you sit so close to me I nearly tell you everything but as usual my timing is crap. Afterwards, we sit in a café not looking at each other and then you say, '*Never mind, love, we'll find somewhere better.*' But we both know it's a lie. Then you say, '*Come home.*'

18. Flashback.

Moose is on the door of the club. Loud music.

STACEY   I love you.

MOOSE   No you don't. Fiver each lads, in you go.

STACEY   I do love you. *(pause.)* No, I don't.

MOOSE   I know. Alright, doll? Danny's inside – So what you gonna do now?

STACEY   Dunno.

MOOSE   Gonna go home?

STACEY   No!

MOOSE   So... where? *(She looks at him.)* No. Didn't I tell you? The only thing –

STACEY   Yeh. You told me.

MOOSE   Nice one. What's your Mum say?

STACEY   Oh, she's over the moon, what d'you think?

MOOSE   Look, I gotta – Alright! Four lovely ladies, welcome to *Hollywood's* my beauties, have a good –

STACEY   Moose – listen...

MOOSE   Sorry mate, not with them trainers on, go home and change then I'll consider it –

STACEY   Moose – I got nowhere to go...

MOOSE   All you had to do was stay in school. And you couldn't even do that for me.

STACEY   No. I couldn't even do that.

MOOSE   Mickey!

Moose goes off. John comes on.

STACEY   What you doing here?

JOHN   Thought I'd find you here. Your Mum asked me to look for you.

STACEY   Buy us a drink then.

JOHN   No chance. Sorry.

Stacey produces a crumpled fiver.

STACEY   I'll get them in then. With my winnings.

JOHN   I'd say Mrs G's the only winner.

STACEY   Can I just say, '*I told you so.*' Always wanted to say
that to a teacher.

JOHN   Congratulations. Look, can we go somewhere a bit
quieter? Have a chat?

STACEY   No. I wanna stay here.

JOHN   You always get your own way, don't you?

STACEY   Oh, yeh.

JOHN   Come on, don't make me beg. *(She smiles.)*
Alright, I'm begging. Please come home?

STACEY   And play happy families? I don't think so.

JOHN   At least for the wedding. It'd mean a lot to
your Mum.

STACEY   And you'd put up with me, for her sake.

JOHN   You're fourteen, Stacey!

STACEY   So? I still ain't /coming home.

JOHN   If you won't /come home –

STACEY   ... and I won't-

JOHN   ... your Mum and me may have to make you a Ward
of Court. I mean we don't want to, but come on, you've been
expelled, you're living with a man like him... For Christ's sake,
what sort of people would we be, if we didn't do something?

STACEY   OK. I'll make you a deal.

JOHN   I'm not doing deals with you.

STACEY   You might do this one. *(She edges closer to him.)*
I'm going to tell you something. When I've told you, I'm going to
go away and never come back. And you're going to go home and
tell my Mum that I'm fine and I'll be in touch. I think I'll have
the flu on the wedding day, but I'll send a card. I'll call her when
I can and you'll make her see that it's for the best.

JOHN   Why the hell would I do that?

STACEY *(moves even closer.)* Because if you don't, I'll go into school tomorrow and I'll tell the head that when you and me were seen in here tonight, you tried it on with me. And I mean *seen.* *(He follows her gaze.)* Yeh, they're all from year eleven. In fact they're in your class. See... you always thought I never listened to you, but you said to me, if you're smart, you'll tell the head it was Mrs G's fault. And I said, who'd believe me? And you said; everyone. Remember? *(She pushes him away, gently. He's in shock.)*

19. Present Time.

STACEY   I kept wishing I had a Stacey who would stop me, make me shut up before it's too late. But there wasn't anyone. Just the throb of the music and the glittery stares of the year eleven girls as I told him, 'I'm pregnant and I'm going to London.' And I think even then if he'd of said the right thing I might have... I don't know... I thought he'd do what I said because... he had no choice. But anyway, he didn't say the right thing, he just stumbled out of the club suddenly looking a lot older but I didn't care, not then. I had no idea what I'd started. And it's getting louder; tick tock, tick tock.

Stacey goes off.

20.
Kandi outside school. Nick comes on, bruised.

KANDI   You're late. What's up with your face, man? You look well scuffed. *(She tries to examine him.)*
NICK   Get off.

Stacey arrives.

KANDI   Who won?
NICK   Nobody won. Can I – ?

KANDI   Which means you didn't, right. I would never let anybody beat me I am tellin' you, I would have more self-respect. Who was it?

NICK   Kandi, can I – ?

KANDI   Was it Jacko?

NICK   ... kiss you?

KANDI   Yeh. Whatever.

She takes her gum out and they kiss quickly. Kandi puts her gum back in.

KANDI   I'm gonna have to have him for this.

NICK   It's not your problem-

Stacey freezes Kandi. She eyes Nick.

STACEY   Listen, *who won?* means, don't make me fight your battles. She's got enough of her own, alright? Try again.

Nick is gobsmacked. Stacey unfreezes Kandi and rewinds.

KANDI   Who won?

He kisses her assertively. Afterwards, he takes her gum out of his mouth. It's a proper kiss.

NICK   Wow.

KANDI   That was alright. I hated being away from school.

NICK   From me?

KANDI   Yeh. Even though I hate school.

NICK   I wish you were in my class this afternoon.

KANDI   Yeh... Is Jacko in that class?

NICK   Yeh, so?

KANDI   Does that hurt?

She presses his bruise.

NICK   Ow! Yeh!

KANDI   Sorry. He done you pretty bad, didn't he?

NICK   No.

KANDI   Yeh he did. I mean I can kick off right? but he's out of order. We're gonna have to sort it out.

NICK   No way, it's my problem.

KANDI   No, we're like a... team. Yeh. We're a team.

NICK   Don't get in trouble again, you've only got –

KANDI   ... five days, yeh, but this counsellor, right... she's like, now you're seeing me, they'll be more patient with you.

NICK   Leave it, alright? Alright?

KANDI   You wanna go *Hollywood's* tonight?

NICK   We ain't gonna get in there!

The bell goes.

KANDI   Yeh we are. You wanna?

NICK   Alright.

KANDI   Gum.

Nick gives her the gum back; she puts it in her mouth, blows him a kiss and he walks off. Stacey appears.

STACEY   What the hell are you playing at?

KANDI   I ain't playin', man. Where were you when I needed you? Nowhere!

STACEY   You can't just call me whenever you feel like it. Only when you really, really need me.

KANDI   You're showing me up. People are looking, I'm talking to myself.

STACEY   Put your *Walkman* on. That way they'll think you've got a hands-free mobile.

KANDI   Cool.

Kandi puts her Walkman headphones in.

KANDI   I've got to go to class.

STACEY   You're up to something.

KANDI   So?

STACEY   Whatever it is, you're going to come off worse. Am I wasting my precious time?

KANDI   Dunno. I don't even know what you're doing here or who you are or why you're so precious.

STACEY   So ask me.

KANDI   How old are you?

STACEY   Twenty-eight.

KANDI   You got a boyfriend?

STACEY   No.

KANDI   Why not?

STACEY   Don't want one.

KANDI   Why can't anyone else see you?

STACEY   Maybe they can.

KANDI   Oh. I thought you said I was special.

STACEY   Too special to get involved with Nick's problems.

KANDI   Maybe I love him.

STACEY   Do you?

KANDI   I might... You gonna tell me I don't know what love is, at my age?

STACEY   No. I'm not going to tell you that.

KANDI   You got kids?

STACEY   No.

KANDI   Did you like school?

STACEY   Not much.

KANDI   You got a job?

STACEY   Yeh. Trying to keep you out of trouble. The bell's gone. Go to class.

KANDI   No! Don't you dare just disappear like that! Stacey!

Stacey freezes Kandi.

STACEY   I can just hear you, Mum. If you tell the truth, we can sort it out. If you lie – no one'll ever know how you felt, will they? It'll be too late.

Stacey unfreezes Kandi.

21. Rewind.

KANDI   You got kids?
STACEY   Yeh.
KANDI   Yeh? How many?
STACEY   One. A boy.
KANDI   Does he see his Dad?
STACEY   No.
KANDI   I don't see my Dad.
STACEY   That's a shame. How come?
KANDI   I'm gonna be late. *(Beat)* Dunno. I think he wants to see me but it's like it reminds him of my Mum and he... just can't have it and I miss him *bad* but look I gotta go –
STACEY   Kandi – just don't –
KANDI   What?
STACEY   Just take care. Be careful. *(Kandi goes.)* Tell the truth. I told half, sometimes that's wiser. I'm trying to make my way toward you Mum but I keep getting snagged on Kandi like wool on a wire. I know what she's going to do. I can't see into the future, I don't need to. She's doing what I would do. Why do you think I chose her? But pay attention. Here's Johnny Bridegroom!

22. Flashback.
John stands up with a glass in his hand. He's half-pissed and dressed in a suit. His tie is off.

JOHN   I'd like to say a few words. I know I'm not the man most of you had hoped to see standing here today. I apologise for that. I'm probably the complete opposite of Stacey's Dad; I hope so. And I hope that doesn't offend Diane or Stacey – Stacey's not here, is she? No. Stacey's having a different kind of celebration to this. I just want to reassure you all that Stacey is fine, she's absolutely fine, and we wish her all the best with the baby. *(Beat)* And hope they'll come home soon. I'd like to make a toast. Raise your glasses!

John wanders off with his glass. Stacey takes his glass.

STACEY   Cheers.

23. Present Time

STACEY   For a long time after that, I was far, far away, in Staceyworld. Later. I've got work to do before I leave and the clock is ticking, remember. Tick tock bang, tick tock bang.

24.
Kandi is standing alone by a cupboard.

KANDI   How you doing, Jacko? Having trouble breathing in there?

There's a violent reaction from the cupboard.

KANDI   No point in shouting, nobody knows you're here. It's your own fault. If you hadn't followed me down here cause you thought I'd give you one, if you weren't such an animal you wouldn't be here –

Kandi kicks the cupboard hard. A yelp. Shouting comes from the cupboard. Muffled, not properly heard, it roughly goes:

JACKO   You fuckin' slut – nobody gives a fuck about you –

KANDI   Yeh, yeh, you dare say this to me because you're in
there. You come out, I'll kill you, man, I'll have to, you know
what I'm sayin'.

JACKO *(in cupboard)* Do it, stupid bitch, do I care?

KANDI   Fine. You know what? I'm gonna let you out. I
wanna see your face when I let you out and I beat the crap out of
you because you're like all the rest.

JACKO *(in cupboard)* I never touched you!

KANDI   Funny, innit, I'm the one who's gonna get kicked
out for this?

Nick comes on.

NICK   Hi.

KANDI   Surprise, right, guess what?

Kandi kicks the cupboard hard.

JACKO *(in cupboard)* Ow! *(Kandi laughs.)*

NICK *(goes to the cupboard)* Jacko?

JACKO *(in cupboard)* You're dead. *(Nick backs off.)*

KANDI   Kick it. Go on.

NICK   No.

KANDI   I got him here for you. *(She kicks the cupboard.)*

JACKO *(in cupboard)* Ow! Let me out!

KANDI   See? *(She kicks it again.)*

JACKO *(in cupboard)* Ow.

NICK   Don't!

Kandi kicks it again.

JACKO *(in cupboard)* Ow.

KANDI   Why not?

NICK   It's only gonna make him worse!

KANDI   Jacko, you feelin' like bullying anyone?

JACKO *(in cupboard)* I just want to go home.

KANDI   Aah. In't he sweet? He wants to go home.

NICK   So do I. What a shame! You can't go home, can
   you?

KANDI   No, he can't go home, not just yet. He's in detention.
   With us.

*They look at each other. They kick hell out of the cupboard,
laughing, catching the buzz off each other.*

NICK   Enough. Let him out now.

KANDI   No way man, I'm just gettin' started.

But the door of the cupboard opens. Stacey comes out.

STACEY   Didn't I say be careful?

NICK   Yeh, but –

BOTH   You can see her?

NICK   /Yeh, she –

KANDI   /You said I was special!

STACEY   I said *be careful*. I said *take care* but you didn't, did
   you?

Nick and Kandi and Stacey look at each other.

JOHN   Oh God. What do we do now?

KANDI   No problem cos Stacey can just rewind it all.

A long beat.

KANDI   Innit, Stace, I made a mistake?

STACEY   Did you?

KANDI   Yeh man, come on.
STACEY   So you put Jacko in a box by mistake?
KANDI   No, but I mean –
STACEY   Or you kicked hell out of the box by mistake?
What did you mean to do then? I don't understand which bit is the
mistake. Help me out here, Kandi, 'cause time is ticking away.

A beat. Nick inspects the inside of the box.

NICK   What I don't get... is... where Jacko is now.
STACEY   In the Headmaster's office.
KANDI   No way. He'd never make such a tit of himself.
STACEY   You sure about that?

Kandi and Nick try to guess if she's bluffing.

KANDI   You're lying.

Stacey snaps her fingers. Moose appears.

MOOSE   Your time's up, girl. The Head wants to see you –
and you. Now. Well go on! What you waitin' for, divine intervention? You – Nick – what's the matter with you, gettin'
involved with /this –
KANDI   /Alright I believe you! Stacey! Make it stop!

Moose takes in the name.

KANDI   Stacey!
MOOSE   Stace?

Stacey freezes him. She touches his immobile face.

STACEY   I'm sorry, Moose. *(She turns him around gently. He walks away.)*

KANDI   You know him?

STACEY   It's none of your business really, is it?

KANDI   But you don't want him to see you, do you?

NICK   Listen –

KANDI   No, so, if you just, like, wipe it all out, then he'll never know, will he? It'll be just like none of it ever happened.

STACEY   Oh, you've really learned your lesson from me, haven't you Kandi? Shame it's the wrong one.

NICK   Listen. How far back can you go?

STACEY   How far do you want?

NICK   Back to the beginning? Could you go that far?

STACEY   All the way?

KANDI   No, 'cause, you'd miss out some good stuff, and maybe it wouldn't always happen again in the same way... like, y'know, childish things...

NICK   Maybe... but like before I had to come to this dump, that'd be good.

KANDI   Then you wouldn't of met me.

NICK   OK, but if I did things different, I could still meet you and not meet Jacko.

STACEY   Can't do that, I'm afraid. You get the whole package or none of it.

NICK   Way back then, before my Mum and Dad split up. I'd start weight-training dead young so I could be a bully.

KANDI   No, I'd hate you then.

STACEY   How about you?

KANDI   Dunno.

STACEY   Time's running out.

KANDI   Anything. Anywhere. Back to before my Mum got ill. I'd stop it. I'd – I dunno, I'd run away then, never have to – see it, or I'd make my Dad stay, I'd watch him every minute to make sure he didn't give in and leave us with nothing and nobody who gives a toss about us that's where I'd go!

Pause.

STACEY   I can't do that.

KANDI   I know you can't. I ain't askin you to do anything. Let's just get this over with. I don't even care if they kick me out this time. I don't care.

NICK   I do.

KANDI   Yeh, well, it ain't your problem. I did it. It's down to me.

NICK   Unless I say, I did it.

KANDI   Yeh, right.

NICK   They ain't gonna throw me out.

STACEY   Yeh they will.

NICK   Why?

STACEY   Because, by now, Jacko's parents are threatening to sue the school and you personally for sustained injuries and trauma.

NICK   Yeh, well... even if they did, I'm still more likely to get into another school than she is.

KANDI   You'd do that for me?

NICK *(shrugs.)* Yeh.

KANDI   Why? You're mad. Why? You've only known me for... You're off your head! Stacey, innit? Listen to him, he's –

STACEY   Time's right up to the wire now. You can hear it ticking away. Choose, Kandi.

KANDI   Would you still go out with me?

NICK   Yeh... *(Beat)* ... course...

KANDI   But what if Jacko said it was me? I got him down here.

STACEY   So we're gonna go with Nick taking the rap?

KANDI   I dunno –

STACEY   Yes or no, Kandi, yes or no?

Pause.

KANDI	You'd really do this for me?
NICK	Yeh.
STACEY	Kandi?
KANDI	No.
NICK	What's the matter with you?
KANDI	Dunno. *(She goes toward him, he turns away.)*
NICK	Tell her!
STACEY	Leave me out of it.
NICK	If you hadn't interfered we'd /be –
STACEY	/Both kicked out about ten minutes ago. Don't thank me, though.
KANDI	You better go home, or they'll find you here. Go on. Go!

Kandi seizes him for a kiss. She turns to Stacey.

KANDI	'Scuse us!

Stacey turns away. They kiss. Nick goes.

KANDI	Come on then.
STACEY	I'm not coming.
KANDI	Oh. Right. *(Beat)* I ain't gonna see you again, am I?
STACEY	Who knows?
KANDI	Yeh.

Kandi turns to leave. She's really scared.

KANDI	D'you think... I'll be alright? I mean after. In the... future, like when I'm older. Think I'll ever be alright?
STACEY	I think you're alright now.
KANDI	No one else does.
STACEY	Nick does.
KANDI	Yeh.

STACEY	Hey. I want you to do something for me.
KANDI	What?
STACEY	Let me go.
KANDI	What d'you mean?
STACEY	Snap your fingers and I'll be gone.

Pause.

STACEY	Snap your fingers, Kandi.
KANDI	I might... I might need you.
STACEY	You're alright. I told you.
KANDI	Yeh, but... I'll never see you again, will I?
STACEY	No. *(She smiles.)* Let me go. I can't go until you let me, see.
KANDI	Where you goin'?
STACEY	Uh... Home.
KANDI	Where's that?
STACEY	Just round the corner.
KANDI	So why d'you have to go now?
STACEY	I'm already late.
KANDI	Like, really, late?
STACEY	Like, *really* late. *(Kandi holds her fingers together.)* Just do it. *(Kandi snaps her fingers.)*

25. Rewind.
Stacey rewinds the scene.

STACEY	I don't know why I'm doing this.

Kandi goes to the cupboard.

KANDI	How you doin', Jacko? Having trouble breathin' in there?

Jacko shouts something. Kandi kicks the cupboard then dithers.

26. Present Time.
Stacey comes on.

STACEY   I'm two hundred yards away from your front door, Mum, but it might as well be another country. And I still feel like the fourteen year old who let you down. Hundred and fifty yards and I'm about to turn the corner and see *Hollywood's*. Just like nothing's changed.

Moose stands outside the club. Stacey watches him.

MOOSE   Ladies, have a good time.

Kandi jumps the queue, strutting up.

KANDI   How's it goin?
MOOSE   Alright.
KANDI   You gonna let me in?
MOOSE   You?
KANDI   Me.
MOOSE   No queue. No hassle about how you're dressed.
KANDI   Yeh.
MOOSE   You're way too young. *(Pause.)* Go on. *(Kandi kisses his cheek.)* That's out of order.
KANDI   Why?
MOOSE   'Cause it is.
KANDI   That was from Stacey.
MOOSE   What? *(He catches Kandi's wrist.)* What the hell are you talkin' about?
KANDI   She just said, 'give him a kiss for me.' Later. *(She goes through the door.)*
MOOSE   Stace? *(Beat)* Stacey?

STACEY   All I've got to do now is to walk up to him, and say his name, and then he'll see me. Anyone can see me if they really want to. But you have to really, really want to. Not just a little bit.

She moves away from Moose. Nick comes over to him, hesitantly.

NICK   Is Kandi – uh – *(Beat)* – you seen her?

MOOSE   In there, mate.

NICK   Yeh... Could you give her a message?

Moose opens the door to him as Kandi comes out.

KANDI   Nick!

Stacey freezes them.

STACEY   Look at them. Look at them, now. How am I going to replay this one? This is going to be one hell of a scene. We can go back, we can go forward, we can just take it from here and see what happens. I'm only one hundred and fifty yards away from you now, Mum, and even if you've gone to bed, I can wake you, can't I? I can wake you both up. John will open the door, and he'll look tired, and old, and you'll call down the stairs, 'Who is it, Johnny?' and he'll say – *(She looks at Moose, Kandi and Nick.)* He'll say, 'Come and see for yourself.' And you'll take your time, I know you – I knew you, and you'll come down, and you'll look at me. You'll look at me. And we'll take it from there.

Lights down.

The end.

Anna Reynolds

A playwright and screenwriter. Her past work has included the multi-award-winning *Jordan,* produced internationally, *Red* for Clean Break Theatre Company, *Precious* for West Yorkshire Playhouse, *Wild Things* for Salisbury Playhouse / Paines Plough and an award-winning short film, *The Winding Sheet,* for Channel 4. Recent work has included: *Skin Hunger* for BAC, (Time Out Critic's Choice Season), *A Certain Age,* a feature film about a young girl and her dysfunctional family, adapted from the best-selling novel by Rebecca Ray, in development with Welsh Screen (Sgrin Wales). She is currently under commission to Watford Palace Theatre for *Ring Road Tales,* a collaborative, multi arts piece with 60 young people from the Watford area, due to be produced in November 2003 and working with *Pursued By A Bear* Theatre Company on a collaborative piece for schools, *Loved.* She also runs a popular website for writers: www.writewords.org.uk

Gorgeous

Gorgeous

I wrote this play as one of a series of projects over many years which have compelled me again and again towards exploring what our women bodies *mean*. This has led me into exploring a range of themes of *extremis:* prostitution, infertility, hysteria. Hysteria at its most basic definition is the conversion of an abreaction to trauma into non-organic physical symptoms – paralyses, deafness, blindness, hallucinations. It reached its peak in the late 19th century with the frenzied displays of *grande hysterie* in Paris which motivated Freud to research his 'talking therapy', evolving into psychoanalysis as we know it. Hysteria is a term no longer in usage in medicine today, although *anorexia nervosa* and eating disorders remain acknowledged hysterical conditions. The anorexic body produces visible symptoms which speak of fears: of being too big, too sexual, too *present*.

Anorexics today are becoming younger, boys are getting it, and the condition is spreading beyond white middle-class high-achieving families. Clearly, cultural ideals regarding perfection have a lot to answer for. The fashion for being thin is where it might start, but it takes a lot more than vanity to starve yourself to death. Eating disorders are nothing if not the manifestation of grim determination, the ability to see an idea through to its end, with death as its tragic consequence for some. Such willpower is manifest too in the bulimic's gorging and vomiting, even if here the flesh speaks less visibly.

I wanted to write about a girl disorientated by womanhood and all its pressures, a journey into herself and her own shifting body image through time. *Gorgeous* is inspired by Virginia Woolf's *Orlando* – who travels in time and gender, Beckett's Winnie in *Happy Days* – stuck menopausally in the engulfing earth – and of course Lewis Carroll's Alice who steps through the real to the other side and becomes herself a shapeshifter.

I wrote the first draft in Princeton, citadel of the achieving academic young woman. The how-to-eat-a-lettuce-in-the-loo episode was shared with me by a brilliant, eating disordered, student. *Gorgeous* has a contemporary young woman in mind. Hence the objects, brand names and slang in this text should be adapted for any production and context.

Anna Furse

Gorgeous
A journey of the body

Anna Furse

The play was first performed in October 1999, at Mount Carmel School, London N19. Directed by Rosamunde Hutt. Design concept by Anna Furse and design collaborator – Suzanne Langston-Jones.

ALICE, a young woman, just turned 15	**Viss Elliot**
VOICES including:	**Viss Elliot**
FUTURE ALICE	
MOTHER	
BARBIE	
RUBY	
FERAL CHERYL	
HANDS, which communicate with Alice and manipulate the objects of her journey	**Marijke Zwart**

Production Manager – Jane Mackintosh
Composer – Graeme Miller
Company Stage Manager – Marijke Zwart
Voice Consultant / Education Resources – Bernadette O'Brien
Dressmaker – Anna von Maltzahn
Accent Advice – Jan Haydn Rowles
Graphic Design – Iain Lanyon
Production Photography – Timothy Nunn

Theatre Centre gratefully acknowledged financial assistance from The Milly Apthorp Charitable Trust, BBC Children in Need, Help a London Child and NatWest Bank for this production.

Notes:

*Hands should appear from inside and under Alice's dress so that
they connect with her own body.*
*(Ruby and Feral Cheryl are both actual dolls. Ruby was
manufactured by the Bodyshop but never marketed. Feral Cheryl is
available via the internet and is used here with the permission of the
doll's creator, Lee Duncan.)*
*One actress played all the voices in the original production but these
could equally be played by several performers.*
*Audience enter to: Alice in a huge pink and white rosebud crinoline
dress which forms the entire stage setting. Her floor-length hair
cascades in curls about her shoulders. The image is prettiness
incarnate, doll-like, ultra-feminine, mysterious and theatrical. This
enormous dress, which remains fixed throughout, serves as a surface
at waist height for the performer to use to manipulate objects, lean,
sleep on – as if it were a table. This surface now bears a book with a
clasp, a quill pen and inkstand. Later, we will discover that the
surface, as well as the dress itself, in fact consists of many apertures
through which Alice will find - or be confronted with - various
objects, dolls, foodstuffs, cosmetics etc.*
All the other characters' voices speak through Alice.

1.

The sound of birds chirping. Alice is asleep. Lightly snoring.
*As the performance begins, an eerie piano plays (Chopin?) which
mutates to the sound of a quill pen scratching on paper. This
corresponds to the action onstage - Alice slowly comes to life.
She is writing her journal.*

ALICE   Dear diary, today is my birthday! And the first day
of Spring. Everything outside is quite bursting with life. Clean
green shoots are pushing up through the earth and there's buds on
the willows furry as newborn kittens. The cherry tree is frothing
with blossom and the river is nearly bursting its banks. I feel...
quite light-headed. And curiously hot. I ran with joy - well, tried
to, only my shoes got caked in mud and the hem of my skirt too
and then I tripped and fell flat on my face and the whole of me

was oozing with the wet brown stuff. So I turned back and tried to avoid Mother but she caught me on the stairs and said

MOTHER'S VOICE Alice Goodbody!! You are a disgrace! When will you learn young lady that you are no longer a child! You are 15!! You cannot cavort about like some unbroken pony. You must learn to be more ladylike. Restraint Alice! Restraint! Or no man will ever wish to marry you! Go upstairs immediately and change your clothes. Put your muddy ones straight into cold water and scrub! And I want to see them hanging on the line within the hour. Leave your shoes till the mud dries and then brush it off. They are probably ruined. But if you keep your skirts over your feet as you are supposed then no one need know. Be off with you! And do your hair!

ALICE   So you see, dear Diary I am a disgrace. I shall never learn to be a proper woman. I shall be on the shelf. Like Auntie Zarie. Unmarried and dependent on my brother to take care of me. Sewing. Trying to make myself useful round the house. But basically *useless*. No parties, no dancing, no swooning. No babies, because the stork only brings them to married girls. I shall just get tighter and tighter and drier and drier until one by one my teeth fall out and... Oh but how can I talk so of Auntie Zarie whom I love and who has been so good to me. Almost like a mother. Grrrrr! I try to be good and quiet and still like Mother says. But then I get this urge to move to run to shout and laugh out loud. I still want to climb trees and lift my skirts to jump over streams... Ouch! *(She suddenly clutches her belly)* What was that? Twinge... ache... it feels like something is dragging me, pulling me down... it's gnawing now, tugging and gnawing... and my back hurts...

MOTHER *(as if calling from another room in the house)* Alice! Have you washed your dress?

ALICE *(shouting as if to another room)* Yes Mother!

MOTHER   And what are you doing now?

ALICE *(hurriedly snapping her diary shut and hiding it and the inkwell, pen)* I... I'm getting ready... I'm doing my hair Mother. I'm trying to plait it and pin it up like you showed me... *(She frantically begins to do this)*

MOTHER   Good. Remember, it is more becoming and practical coiled tight and then pulled over the ears. You don't need to fuss with it then.

ALICE   Yes Mother!

MOTHER   Oh and Alice!?

ALICE   Mother?!

MOTHER   Remember, God is watching you!

ALICE *(fearful now, cowering, eyes upwards)* Yes Mother...

2.

Alice has finished her hair and has furtively taken out her journal again. She writes.

ALICE   Dear Diary, I resolve: not to be a disgrace to my family. Henceforth I will not rush about. I will not lose a sense of restraint. I shall be dignified. I shan't talk about myself or my feelings to anyone (except you). I shall interest myself more in others and put my own interests second. I shall think before speaking. I shall work seriously. I shall be restrained... I shall, I shall, both in conversation and in my actions... I shall try to think before speaking and speak before doing. I shall not let my thoughts wander. I shall try not to be clumsy and boyish. I shall strive to be ladylike. I shall. I wish to improve myself for the sake of my Mother, a widow and a brave and resourceful woman, and all she has done for me in teaching me to be a woman and helping me to approach my adulthood with grace and virtue – oops! Oh heavens! *(She has knocked the inkwell in her writing fervour. It has spilt on her dress. She looks helplessly at her inky fingers resists the impulse to rub them on her dress, admits that she has, again, messed up and wails)* Oh I will try, I will, hear me God! It was an accident... Ohhhhhh!!!

3.

Suddenly a pair of hands appear from within the tabletop. They are proferring a white sanitary towel. Alice, alarmed but curious, dabs at it. The hands beckon. They are saying, "Use this". Alice gingerly wipes her hands on the towel which is now stained blue. Suddenly the magic hands swipe it away and close the lid so that the table is as it was before.

ALICE   Curiouser and curiouser. I thought... Oh my
goodness! Oh... I thought... It looked just like... only Mother's
are... cotton cloth. I know because I've seen them on washdays
and asked about them and she told me I might soon be wearing
them too. When *(with great difficulty)* my m-e-n-a-r-c-h-e comes.
(whispering) Eve's curse. The sweet secret. I mean... maybe it
wasn't... Oh! The shape, oh goodness, oh... Dear God! *(flustered,
scribbles in her diary)* I *think* I have just started my – I think I
have just become – I believe I have just passed the threshold from
girlhood to womanhood – I... Oh gracious! This is the menstrual
'flower' Mother has warned me about. She told me about how
like flowers we are. How we need this, this 'issue', so as to
become mothers ourselves. Oh. My hands are shaking! Ow! As I
look out of the window I see the lilacs blooming. Just as I have
been told they do. They, bloom and fade. They produce flowers,
and then fruit and then seeds which scatter to be... to... to enter the
earth once more in order to germinate and make roots downwards
and shoots upwards. Oh my goodness! I'm perspiring! What shall
I tell Mother? She will now, for sure , restrict my diet. No more
pickles, meat or cloves, for fear they excite me. Oh, I am so
frightened. And I hurt. My lower region is aching. I think I want
to lie down. Drink tea. Do nothing. I have a headache! I feel sick.
And so huge. As if I had drunk a barrel of water. Maybe I can
skip my tea party. I shall say that I am... indisposed. From now on
I shall mark this occasion simply with the letter "X".
*(Hands appear from another part of the table top. They offer
Alice a booklet. NB this should be a sex education manual as
currently used in schools. Alice takes it and reads it out loud.
Her eyes grow wide.)*
No! It can't be possible! I cannot believe that there can be such
things! *(reads)* Oh gracious! There's even a diagram of – No.
No!!!!! This is surely not for my eyes. I can't look! "Tam-pon".
What on earth? It looks so – unpleasant. So peculiar. Like a
telescope. No! Not right. It can't be right. No I could never,
never, I think I'll be sick! Ohh... *(flicks the pages and scrutinises*

the back cover) "... copyright 2003!"
(She gasps in horror, throws the booklet. Hands catch it. Make it vanish. Hands produce a large watch. A time-travelling cacophony of ticking and whirring during which Alice moves her upper body as if she is tumbling (cf Alice in Wonderland's fall.) During this Hands throw up various objects, pieces of clothing from different apertures in the tabletop. When this is over, the table is strewn with teenage girl objects of fetish. Alice surveys them one by one. She picks up a magazine with a picture of Di Caprio.)
"Leonardo - true love, the true story" *(She picks up a pair of Calvin Klein women's boxer short knickers. Admires them.)*
I think Mother might approve of these. Well, they're grey. Cotton. Unadorned. Except perhaps they're a bit short... Maybe they belong to someone very small. *(reads)* "C.A.L.V.I.N. K.L.E.I.N" Hmm. That doesn't sound like a girl. *(drops them)* Ooooh! Maybe they're not girls'. Oh! What if they're boys'. *(picks them up very fearfully and reads the label again)* "One size. Washing instructions: machine wash forty and tumble dry? "Machine???? Tumble??? Why would Calvin want anyone to know these things about herself, or himself? *(She picks up a pair of platform shoes)* Oooooh. I've seen pictures of these in my book about Greek Drama. *(picks up a Wonderbra)* What on earth could this be? *(finds label and reads)* "Wonderbra" what a strange word. "Thirty-four B cup"... must be some cooking thing. For measuring ingredients? Maybe for cheese-making? You could put the curds in here and hang it over... Certainly couldn't drink out of it. Feels nice. Reminds me of something but I cannot think what. *(finds a make-up purse)* Ah! I know what this is. Well, at least I think I do - no, maybe not... *(She opens lipsticks, blushers, eyeliners, mascaras and reads all the names and descriptions, puzzled and very interested e.g.)* "Titian Red", "Charcoal", "Irridescent Rose Madder"... Maybe it's some artist's bag. Wait a minute. *(opens a powder compact)* I think I know what this might be *(she sniffs it, dabs her fingers on it, crumbles it in her fingers)* Yes! I knew it! Powder paint!! Maybe Calvin is an artist. Maybe Leonardo is Leonardo Da Vinci and Calvin is his pupil... Maybe Calvin helped mix the colours for the Mona Lisa! Maybe he fell in love with her! But why the knickers? *(finds a mobile phone)*

Gracious! What extraordinary material. Sort of like coal. No.
Iron. No. I've never felt anything quite like it. Oh! It's got
numbers on it! *(She explores the keys, accidentally punches a
stored number and gets through).*
FUTURE ALICE Hello. This is Alice's mobile voicemail. Please
leave a message after you hear the beep, saying who you are and
when you called and I'll get back to you when I can. Bye.
ALICE *(amazed)* It, it can't be – it sounds so familiar.

*Alice slams the phone down. Then cautiously picks it up and tries
again. This time, after the voicemail message comes on again:*

FUTURE ALICE Hello. This is Alice's mobile voicemail. Please
leave a message after you hear the beep, saying who you are and
when you called and I'll get back to you when I can. Bye.
ALICE Who are you? Are you in there? Can you hear me?!
I'm Alice. I'm Alice Goodbody. And I'm very confused. I'm
fifteen years old. Well, just. Today is actually my birthday. I'm
just getting ready for my tea-party to celebrate. I have just turned
fifteen. Just now. About to – I have just had the most extraordinary sensation of falling. Everything looks just the same, only
different somehow. I'm the same. My dress is the same, my hair
is the same (well same but different. I mean. Oh never mind...)
everything's the same. Only there are all these strange objects
strewn around and, well, I am, well, feeling unwell, a little...
unwell, I can't really talk about it but let's just say I'm indisposed. A woman who is indisposed. A woman, yes, woman. Young
woman, er, as it were, well, maybe that's why I feel so confused.
Maybe that's why I feel like I have fallen. I don't know who you
are but I feel I know you. If you're a ghost I'm not frightened of
you. Surprisingly. So maybe you'd like to put the matter straight
and make yourself known to me. I'm here now. I'm not going
anywhere, so I think you'll find me. Here, where I always am –

*There's a loud tone and then a click. Alice has run out of message
time. She doesn't understand this. She's puzzled.*

4.

Suddenly the phone in her hands rings. She's alarmed. She explores it as if it were an archeological find. Trying to understand what the noise is and its provenance. Then, by accident, discovers the answer button. Future Alice's voice now speaks:

FUTURE ALICE Alice! Hiya! It's me. Got your message. It's wicked to hear you. I've been like doing this project at school and and I've been thinking what it must be like to be living like a hundred years ago and now... you've arrived! Oh innit such a *relief* we got our period at last?! I was nearly the last in the class. I really thought there was something wrong with me. D'you know what I mean? I'm well happy I've come on. I want everyone to know, everyone! I can't wait to tell the girls at school. They'll stop calling me fried eggs now innit. D'you know what I think? I think they should throw a party for us to celebrate. I do! Shani at school says that in Ghana the Asante tribe put a girl who's just started under an umbrella and sing and dance in her honour. What do we get? A lesson in hygiene and a packet of *Lillets*. It's well out of order! Well from now on I'm going to have big tits and wear a push up *Wonderbra* on Saturday nights! Mind you right now they feel like someone's been using them for boxing training so maybe I'll leave it a week! Oh it's so cool to hear you! Welcome to the future. We are going on a journey into our womanhood. Oi you know like you found our knickers and make-up? What you thought was paint? It's face paint... make-up, you know? Well, you probably don't but never mind. The "cheese-cloth"? That's a bra. Size thirty-four bust means we're not exactly Posh Spice but we're, well, sort of sporty.

ALICE   Size? What do you mean? I don't have a size. I'm just me.

FUTURE ALICE So where d'you get your clothes from, and how do you know what size to buy? Hm?

ALICE   I or Mother, make my clothes by hand.

FUTURE ALICE Wow. So like you'll never know if you're 'the wrong size'. That's sooooo cool. I like it. I hate sizes. And manufacturers seem to make them up as they go along anyways so shopping can be a nightmare. D'you know what? Half the time I want to rave all night in my platforms and the other half I want to curl up in Mum's lap sucking my thumbs and have her feed me bowls of sticky toffee pudding. There's so much pressure. To look great. To do well at school so as like to get a job or even go to college. To attract boys. Safe sex –

Alice shrieks and drops the phone. She starts gagging.

FUTURE ALICE *(whispering)* Alice! Relax. I know. That word. Scary eh? We're terrified of it all– Terrified that our skin's breaking out. Acne. Spots. Blackheads. Ugh! And hair. In the wrong places. Bikini lines, and legs and armpits and face! And blood. Terrified of this bleeding. That it might show. Terrified of changing, of being touched, of having to get it on with boys so that our schoolmates think we're really cool. Terrified of being different. Of not fitting in. Of being lonely and left out. Of our parents finding out what we get up to. Of them stopping us. Stopping my pocket money. Stopping us going out. Going with our mates. Terrified of our mates. Terrified of being laughed at for our boobs, our bum, our legs, our nose, our hair, our mouth, our teeth, our face. Terrified of being dissed. Of being crap at school. Of people thinking I'm not clever. Of what I'm gonna do with my life. Of not getting a job. Of getting a job. Of getting married. Of not getting married. Of getting pregnant...

ALICE   Yes! Yes! Yes!

FUTURE ALICE You know what we need right now?

ALICE *(into the mouthpiece)* What?

FUTURE ALICE A cheeseburger and chips and a large *Coke*.

ALICE   A what?

FUTURE ALICE Whenever I get like this I just need to eat.

ALICE   I don't know what you're talking about. The cheese thingummyjig.

FUTURE ALICE What? Alice! A cheeseburger is the best invention since sliced bread. Ground meat in a bun, cheese on top and fried potatoes... Anyways and you put loads of tomato ketchup on it and it's well nice. I can eat more than one at a go and *Coca Cola* is a fizzy brown drink that tastes... well, I can't describe it... but there's really only one brand that's the real thing.

ALICE   I want some!

5.

Hands produce a complete burger meal on a plastic tray. There is a big sign on it: EAT ME. DRINK ME. Alice is fascinated. Starts to eat and drink. Guzzles. Makes approving sounds and speaks with her mouthful:

ALICE   Gracious me this is good!!!! Mother wouldn't approve at all! She wants me to stop eating meat for fear it makes me... excited... and as for this sweet beer stuff... it's... so... funny. Feels like I've swallowed a balloon full of air. Oh how do you make this food? Aren't you clever! I want the recipe. Let me write it down now. *(takes her diary and pen)*

FUTURE ALICE Fast food Alice! Junk food, fast food, quick and cheap and over-the-counter-I-can't-wait food! I can't give you the recipe! It's a trade secret! Remember Alice, this is nearly the 21st century! Food's ready to eat. You just buy it that's all. You just walk in and buy it.

ALICE   You mean I don't have to learn how to cook?

FUTURE ALICE Nope. Not really. Except a bit of microwaving I s'pose...

ALICE   So what do I do all day if I'm not planning and preparing meals?

FUTURE ALICE *(laughs)* I dunno. Live your own life. Dream your dreams...

ALICE   Of perfection?!!

6.

This thought disturbs Alice. Hands produce a mirror. Alice takes it and scrutinises her face.

ALICE   Eurgh! A blemish! Another one! Oh no! Blackheads! My face is so... fleshy!! Pudgy! I've never really looked at it

closely before! *(pinches her cheeks, under her chin)* I'm ugly!
(scans the rest of her upper body with the mirror) disgusting. This
dress is too tight! I hate myself! I hate myself! I want blue eyes!
No green! No brown! No grey! I want to be fair-skinned! No
dark! I want to be taller! No shorter! I want straight hair, curly
hair, black hair, blonde hair! I want bigger boobs, smaller boobs,
no boobs. I want a flat stomach! I want... I want... I want another
cheeseburger!
(Hands produce another tray of food. This time there's a Sundae.)
On second thoughts, I want you, whatever you are, soft pink
creamy sweet pudding that you are! Mmmmmmmm...

*Alice eats. As she does so, Hands produce a naked Barbie doll. Alice
stops eating, is embarrassed but fixated. The more fixated she is on
Barbie the more she eats. She feels Barbie is watching her.*

BARBIE   A minute on the lips, a lifetime on the hips.

ALICE   I beg your pardon?

BARBIE   It's full-fat ice cream and double whipped cream. It's
a naughty naughty naughty sinful naughty dessert. Are you really
sure you want it?

ALICE   Who are you?

Soupy muzak underscores the following self-advertisement.

BARBIE   Hi! I'm Barbie! Diva of the doll-world. I'm a best-
seller!! Two of me are sold each minute! If you laid all of me in
the world end to end I'd circle the earth seven times! I'm forty-
three years old and I still look as young and pretty and impossible
as I did in 1959. Do you know I was the first doll with breasts? At
first this meant I didn't sell well but then folks got kinda used to
my cute little pointy things and, well, the rest is history. I'm
actually an anatomical impossibility. Like most classical nude
paintings of women as a matter of fact. I mean Botticelli's Venus
couldn't stand up if she tried!! Proportionally my feet are
equivalent to a toddler's shoe-size. And my waist, well, it's even
smaller than those lovely corseted seventeen inchers you gals in

the nineteenth century love so much. The thing about me is my total flexibility. I have had no less than five hundred make-overs in forty years! See I keep up! I'm always NOW! I can adapt my style, my fashion sense, even my ethnicity to whatever the current market might be. Folks can never get enough of me! Kids go wild for me! So does Ken actually. Have you met Ken? He's my bendy-legged toyboy, boytoy, boyfriend, fiancé, husband, colleague…

(Hands produce a naked Ken doll. Alice hides her eyes and peeps through her fingers.)

We've both got our own lives and interests but there's lots we do together. We date all the time. Oh sorry. Ken and I are both real relaxed about nudity, even though we both have such extensive wardrobes. You will note that Ken has no er… real, bump at the front. That's because everybody out there just didn't want the real thing you know. Like I don't have any pubes! I guess that might be one reason why we both keep smiling!!! *(Barbie giggles)* None of that nasty down below stuff to get in the way of a lovely, outfit-filled, hobby-happy life of style and fantasy…

ALICE   It's very nice to meet you but *please* put some clothes on, please!!

BARBIE   Sure!

Hands produce Barbie and Ken outfits. Alice realises she is supposed to do the dressing and does so, deeply curious but ashamed at her interest in their bodies.

ALICE   What on earth are these supposed to be?!

BARBIE   "Hot surfers." My thong bikini sure gets some approval let me tell you and Ken, well, he's just soooooo hot in his bermuda print surfing shorts… *(her voice gets muffled by Alice pulling things over her head)*

ALICE   If Mother could see me now she'd die! Absolutely die! I've never seen a boy naked. Never seen myself naked. It's, it's wrong I mean it's unattractive and should never be allowed. When I get married, my husband will never be allowed to see me naked. Never! I should die of shame! And I never never want to see him in... in... the flesh as it were. I think you are both immoral. I think you have no shame. No sense of decorum and what's proper. I think your 'dating' is quite outrageous. I think you're obscene, outlandish and... and... quite... gorgeous!!! *(Alice throws the dolls down. Hands whips them away.)* Please come back! *(Hands produces an array of Barbies of all ethnicity and styles. Alice handles them all.)* You're all the same really. Same face shape, eyes, everything, just different skin tones. And you're always blonde, whatever the colour of your hair!! Even you *(She picks up an Asian model)* and you *(She picks up a black model)* have the same features. You are cute, all-American, cheesecake white girls. What did I just say? What do those words mean? I look at you *(Hands proffer mirror again)* and then myself. I can only see difference. There's nothing about you that looks like me. I touch your taut limbs, your tiny waist, your tight breasts and you feel like some miniature un-breakable dream of hard body and daintiness. You're a plastic princess. Epic womanhood. You' re everything and everyone and everywhere. I dress you, I dream of the world in which you live, of fun, of appliances and of jobs being all about wearing the right clothes and smiling a lot. *(Alice's voice is now mutating into Future Alice)* When I play with you I'm playing with a dream. A serious dream. A dream of career and boyfriend and wide-eyed beauty. Your beauty is my shame. I'll never be you. I can only admire you. I want more and more of you in my hands. I want to belong to your world. I want to be a part of your world-wide corporation. I'll buy you. I'll dress you. I will I will!! And I will visit your website at www dot Barbie dot com and I will never never stop loving you! I'm so hungry! I'm dying to eat! I need some chocolate now!!!!

7.

Hands produce chocolate. Alice munches, begins to cry.

ALICE   This is hell. I hate being here, being me, here. Sweet sweet creamy melt-on-my-tongue and smell-of-angels food! Can't get enough! What's happening to me?!!!!!!!

BARBIE *(Nurse or doctor doll, smug, treacly)* Chocolate has a chemical in it that replaces the chemical lost in tears when we cry. That's why when you're unhappy you think of chocolate. And when you've got your period you lose a lot of iron. Chocolate contains a lot of iron. So when you have your period and you want to cry and eat chocolate it means you're unhappy and low in both iron and that weep chemical. I guess you could say chocolate and tears well, just go together for women...

ALICE   Shut up!!!!!!!!
(She wallops Barbie on the table to cut her off. She is evidently strung out and screams an enervated scream. When she stops she's astonished and at first delighted. Then she suddenly glances around, nervous.)
Oh I'm so sorry! I don't know what came over me. I just lost control. I'm really truly sorry. Please forgive me. *(shakes Barbie who doesn't speak any more)* Oh goodness! Are you dead?! Are you alive? You're just a doll! I think I'm going mad! I feel a kind of hysteria rising in my throat. Desperate. Alice? Are you there? I need to find myself!! Where am I just when I need myself? *(picks up phone and dials but doesn't get any joy)* Shit! Gracious! Who said that? Gracious oh... I think I'm beginning to see where it's going. Where I'm going. No more other Alice. Just this Alice, this me. Shit shit shit!!! I'm the past and the present all rolled into one. I'm a time-traveller and a shape-shifter. I have a magical body. I'm shifting shape...

Alice is now surrounded with 'dead' Barbies and Kens and some of the detritus of foodstuffs and clothing from before. Chaos in other words.

8.

ALICE   I'm growing! I'm becoming huge! My neck is streeeeetching. My head can touch the ceiling. I can hardly see my feet any more. I'm blowing up now like a hot air balloon. Getting bigger and bigger and bigger. I'm feeling strong now. And powerful. I'm taking up space in the space around me. I'm a huge me. No one can ignore me. No one dare insult me. I'm the life and soul of the party. Everyone loves me. That Alice they say,

she's soooo strong and amazonian. She's a goddess. She's
hilarious. She's invincible. I'm a larger-than-life woman. Really
here. Not floating in some frilly meringue of wispy girlishness.
I'm muscle and strength and deep voiced and earthed and really
connected. No? No? No! No! That's not right? That's not the
story? So what is the story? I get it. I get it now. Oh. OK. This is
big me: no waist, no hips. Just a huge mass of blubber. I'm
disgusting. A wobbling mound of jelly. My flesh hangs in folds
from my chin to my knees. It tumbles, like rolled dough, fold
upon fold, now melting into itself, now separating. My surface is
moist with perspiration. I'm all hot and heavy. My thighs rub
against each other, my buttocks dance a silly bouncing dance
behind me. My face is disappearing into this pudding of fat that's
adding and adding itself like a halo of lard round my eyes and
mouth. I'm all soft and squidgy. A blob. Grotesque. Shapeless. A
human mountain. Fingers vanish into my belly, drown in my own
flesh. My bones are crushing with the weight of me, my volume,
my mass. I am all bulk. I am a rhino an elephant a pig. I'm a pig
I'm a pig I'm a pig!!!!! Nobody loves me. I hate myself!!!!! I've
got to eat!!!!! I'm disgusting! I've got to eat! Something to fill
this emptiness inside! I'm a great guzzling cave! I want to fill up
with food. Stuff myself! Fill every crevice of me with food. Feed
me!! Love me!

All kinds of Voices now taunt Alice who is in a reverie:

VOICES   Fatty!
               Fat slag!
               Bouncing Bertha!
               Lump of lard!
               Have you got someone stuck to you?
               Slimfast works you know, you should try it!
               King Kong!
               Fatgirl!
               Miss Piggy!
               Bigboobs!
               Whales belong in the sea!
               Flubber!

Pigface!
Lazy fat cow!

Alice suddenly breaks out of her reverie.

ALICE   I hate myself! I need to get a grip. Take control.
Show them. You are what you eat. I'm eaten up with hating this.
I'll make them eat their words. Choke on them.
(She cries. Then stops) Soooooooooooo, simple: calorie control is
fat control. From now on I'll count. *(takes diary and mutters as
she writes e.g.)*
Chicken soup (tinned) – one cup . Calories: one hundred and
sixty-seven times two plus –
Potato chips – one ounce serving size two hundred and fifty
calories times three plus –
Burger – regular three ounce serving size, two hundred and
eighty-six calories times three plus –
White bread roll – seventy calories times three plus –
One tablespoon tomato ketchup sixteen calories times three
equals two hundred and fifty plus two hundred and eighty-six
plus seventy plus sixteen times three equals one thousand eight
hundred and sixty-six plus –
One pint chocolate ice cream equals one thousand calories plus
fudge sauce equals three hundred calories equals thirteen hundred
calories plus –
One extra large *Coke,* the real thing, equals a hundred calories –
equals a grand total of... *(stops muttering)* Jesus! I've just
dreamed of eating a pound of flesh!!! What's a pound of flesh?
Three thousand five hundred calories, that's what. OK, start again
Alice. Reduce Alice. Eliminate. Cut down. Lighten. Diminish.
Look for fat-free, sugar-free, low-cal solutions to life. Get it
down! Down! Melt it away. Burn it off. Match input to output. No
increase, output to input. A calorie is a measurement of heat. Cool
down Alice. Take the weight off your legs. Diet. Exercise. Slim.
Trim. Look for a new you. Start today! OK OK.
One cup chicken broth – eighty-one calories.
One burger, no roll, low sugar ketchup – three hundred and fifty
calories.

One low-fat sugar-free yoghurt – one hundred calories.
One *Diet Coke* zero zero zero. Total – five hundred and thirty-
one. There. That's better. Much better. Much more like it. If I just
eat one meal a day like this I'll burn up two thousand calories
which is... *(Pause)* I'm famished!!!

9.
Hands produce Ruby – a voluptuous doll

ALICE   Who are you? You're, you're ridiculous! Yuk!

RUBY *(over sincere)* I'm Ruby. I was made because Barbie is
ridiculous. I'm here to tell you, you look just fine as you are. A
woman's curves, her shape, any shape she chooses, is a natural
part of who she is. Most women don't conform to standard ideals
of beauty as promoted by fashion models and *Barbie* dolls. Most
women are...

Alice can't take this piety.

ALICE   Shut up, will you! I'm on a journey of self-
improvement and no one's going to stop me! I'm losing weight!!
I'm reducing. I'm starting to find my bones again, under my skin.
See? My fingers aren't drowning in blubber. I can just poke my
tummy lightly and it bounces back. I'm a size Twelve, Ten, Eight,
going down. I simply eliminate food. So what I do is first I
fantasise about everything I want to eat. Then I add it all up. Then
I calculate exactly what I can eat each day that's under one
thousand calories. That way I reckon I will lose two thirds of a
pound a day which is roughly five pounds a week which is twenty
pounds a month which is, well, great, just great.

RUBY   Alice, you're beautiful, just as you are...

*Alice pushes Ruby away. Hands produces a lettuce and a bottle of
low-cal/fat-free dressing.*

10.

ALICE   I've begun... I'm melting. It's divine. I love
vanishing! They're starting to praise me out there now. They say,
"Wow! You look great! Really great.'' I see envy in their eyes. It
spurs me on. Here's what I do when I really get into this thing. I
get light headed just talking about it. It makes me feel like I'm
walking on air. High as a kite. Floating away like a puff of
smoke. When I do this I'm an angel. I'm good. I'm reaching for
perfection. I'm in control. I measure time in mouthfuls. My every
minute is devoted to achieving my goal of perfection. See. Here's
some of my very own special recipes. First – 'Turning over new
leaves.' Find a quiet place where you won't be disturbed. A toilet
will do, where you can lock the door and be sure of no interrupt-
ions. Then, sit comfortably, cradling your (washed) lettuce. Open
a bottle of low-cal salad dressing and one by one dip the leaves
into the dressing until you've eaten all the lettuce and drunk the
whole bottle. It's so great! It can take hours. You can really make
it stretch. And it's only a total of two hundred and fifty calories. If
you really really get that kind of I want-something-hot-and-
comforting-and-filling feeling, there's always my what I call 'Do-
it-yourself-hot-pot.' You need a small can of vegetable soup –
one hundred calories – carefully remove all the beans to reduce
the original calorie content of one hundred and thirty, take some
low-sugar breakfast cereal – one cup, a hundred and twenty
calories – and mix it with the soup. Bake in a microwave for
fifteen minutes so that the bottom gets really caked and crunchy
and burnt and the top forms a crust. Remove from microwave and
enjoy picking at this for at least one and a half hours, total
calories two hundred and twenty! Then there's the 'Now-you-
chew-it-now-you-don't.' For this you need a packet of sweet
chewing gum. Chew the sugar out of it and spit. Perfect for those
gnawing sugar-craving moods when you could eat your own arm.
Calories? (no cheating) Zero. And finally 'Raw illusion': slice
one apple, with peel – eighty-one calories – and one stick of
celery – six calories – into tiny shards. Caress these in your mouth
for as long as you possibly can before biting. It's the best and
healthiest and lowest calorie meal you can get away with in this
disgusting world full of food food food where everybody eats and
eats and eats around you. Fat dribbling down their faces! Mouths

full of cake! Chewing and spitting crumbs when they talk. And
laughing with their mouths full! It's repulsive! It shouldn't be
allowed! Not in public! Eating should be a private affair!!

VOICES   Painfully thin!
            Stick insect!
            Boy-girl!
            Skinny!
            Who ate all the salad then!
            Needs sellotape to stick herself together!
            Bone-woman!
            Wasting away!
            Belsen!
            Unwomanly!
            Frigid!
            Thin!
            Bird!
            Skinny!
            Walking skeleton!
            Bone-bag!

ALICE   No! No! Rubbish! You don't understand anything!
You're blind! Use your eyes! Look at me!!!

11.

ALICE *(to audience now)* I'm still fat! Can't you see? I'm still fat
and I need to keep working on improving myself. Anyway. This
way I get to stop my periods which is some relief I can tell you.
And boys stop looking at me like they want to... to... do things
with me. And women admire me. I know they do. They think to
themselves, "I wish I was as in control as Alice. I wish I had her
determination, her willpower." Every time I deny myself
something to eat and they have some I feel great and they feel
guilty. I look at you all and you seem... how shall I put it? Fleshy.
Yes. And it makes me feel so virtuous. And funnily enough it
makes me want to feed you all up even more. It makes me want to
bake for you, little scones and bread and cakes and all those
things I might pretend to eat with you but I'm really spitting into
my napkin or vomiting up afterwards because I can do that too
you know? It's easy that bit. Great for binges. It's always best to

start with something bright and colourful like tomato juice. That way you'll know when you've got it all up. So you start with the colour-marker as it were and then eat and eat and eat, ten thousand calories if you like. Then, it's fingers down throat in the loo and magic!! It's all out and you can forget it ever went in and down in the first place. If you don't like vomiting, laxatives will work almost as well. Except it can be really painful.

MOTHER   Alice if you go on like this you're going to die!!

ALICE   Exercise is the key, Mum. You can always measure the calories you eat against those you use to move about. I never take a lift. I run up stairs. I do push ups and jog for hours each day. The important thing is to keep moving.

MOTHER   Alice, you're killing yourself!

ALICE   I take tablets too. Chemical warfare on my insides. Stuff to make my system speed. Gobble up the calories. Tick tick tick. There's a ball of adrenalin stuck in my throat. Its all go go go!!

MOTHER   Alice! You're dying!

ALICE *(suddenly paying attention to Mother's voice)* I can't anymore! I collapse in the street, faint at school... I've shrivelled to a crisp. I'm dry as a twig. I could snap any moment. I stink! I stink of my disappearing act. My teeth have crumbled. There's baby-hair all over my body. On my face. But the hair on my head's falling out. My skin is dry. It's lost all elasticity, all tone. My bones hurt. They're bruised from sitting and lying. My eyes stare out of my skull like a lemur. They stare at you all and say, "What are you looking at?!" Is this good enough? No. There's no such thing as perfection! I tried I tried I tried! It started because I felt so big. Now I feel so very very small. "You're very small," said the elephant to the mouse. "I know," said the mouse. "I've been ill. " I've been ill. I'm cold all the time. I wear woollen sweaters even in the heat of summer. My teeth chatter. Help, someone, please. I'm terrified of putting on weight, but I know I must. Please talk to me. Talk to me and help me. Help me! I don't want to be a woman! I want to keep away from you all! Hide away! I repulse you, don't I? *(Hands produce magazine. She flips it.)* "Get rid of unwanted flesh fast. Cosmetic surgery may be the answer to your dreams. The Lissom Clinic offers free confidential advice on most types of surgical procedures including liposuction and collagen injections." Yes! Yes! That's the answer! The knife! Suction! Anything! I'll have it cut off, Vacuumed out. I'll have a nose job, ear job, breast job, tummy job, buttock job, thigh job and I'll get my face sorted too. Build up the cheekbones. Get my eyelids pinned. A bit of collagen in the lips. I'll re-model the whole lot of me. Nothing will stop me! Nothing! No one! I want to be gorgeous! I want to be gorgeous! I've got to be gorgeous! Gorgeous! Gorgeous! *(Alice swoons into a kind of trance)*

12.
Hands produce a Feral Cheryl doll. She speaks in an Australian accent.

FERAL CHERYL Hey doll. Get a life. It's OK. You're fine. What's with all this high-tech medical crap hmh? You're gorgeous just as you are you know. And bright. You should try spending more time feeding your brain you know. Beauty's a relative concept. What's in today is out tomorrow. Enjoy yourself while you're still young. Life's too short. There's a wonderful world out there and the future is female!! Look at you sat there all laced-up, wishing you were someone else, dreaming the impossible. Face yourself! You're the product of Western Civilisation's own worst hang-ups: the beauty industry!

ALICE   Who on earth are you?

FERAL CHERYL I'm a friend. I'm Feral Cheryl. I'm thirty-four centimetres tall with brown hair, brown eyes and a realistic body shape. I have pubic hair (why are people so shocked by this?) I am made in Australia in a cottage industry, unlike Barbie who is the product of the Third World sweatshop industry. I represent a simple lifestyle. See? Simple clothing. I don't need that excessive wardrobe and all those accessories. I take my inspiration from people in Australia who work in the rainforest on ecological issues. Touch me. *(reluctantly Alice does so)*

ALICE   You're very confident aren't you?

FERAL CHERYL Dunno. But I guess you could say I'm content with my lot. In control of my life...

ALICE   Lucky you. You'll never catch on, you know. You're
silly. And you sound like my Mum's hippy friend. And I don't
like what you're wearing. People want glamour...

FERAL CHERYL Yeah. I know. But as it happens there's a bit of
a cult-following about me from Manhattan to the Shetland Isles
actually. I have my own website and I've been on TV in London
and in California. So watch it miss smug-features.

ALICE   OK. Really? T.V. Huh... By the way, I really like
those things on your arms. What are they?

FERAL CHERYL Tattoos. Primitive body art. Incredibly
fashionable all over the world. A little bit of pain (quite nice
actually) and the ink goes in the flesh to produce the image of
your choice, permanently.

ALICE   I want one. A snake. On my ankle. And a butterfly
on my shoulder. And a pig on my belly!! No! I've got it! Medusa.
I want Medusa tattooed all over me. Medusa with her head of
coiling snakes. Medusa who was so hideous that people turned to
stone when they looked at her! And I want what you've got
through your ears. What's that?

FERAL CHERYL Pierced my dear. Hey. Maybe you could get
some piercings? Better than all that cosmetic surgery nonsense
any day. This way you get to be the artist and your body is your
canvas. You can re-invent yourself the way you want. Adorn
what's there, don't destroy it. Celebrate your own flesh! Most
people start with ears. But you can get your belly-button done, or
your nose... Oh I could go on... eyes, lips, tongues, and and...

ALICE   Yes, yes, yes, I want to have pierced everything!
I want my tongue full of diamonds. I want my eyes fringed in
rings. I want silver studs all over my ears and my nose. And I
want scars. Beautiful patterns over my eyebrows. I want to suffer
the pain and the ecstasy of needles breaking open my flesh. I want
to feel! I want to feel everything. The blood. Savour the moment I
mark my own flesh, press ink and metal into it, inscribe it with
my own story. I want to own my own body! I want to make
myself mine mine mine! I won't care what people think! They'll
think I'm ugly and stupid anyway. But this way at least they can
admire my guts. "Did Alice really go through all that pain to look
like that!?" Yes! Yes! Yes she will! And I want to emerge from

my ordeal, proud of my endurance. A terrible beauty. The beauty of my power, the power of suffering... I want to be a saint. An angel! *(screams)* Pierce me!! Cut me!! Paint me in needlepoint! My flesh! My flesh! My flesh is me! I want to be free!!!!!!!!!!!!!!

FERAL CHERYL Hey doll! Come back! Wake up and smell the big beyond. Eat the wind! Drink the sea! Let your hair down. Put on your dancing shoes. Like you could go backpacking, you know. See the world. Sunset in Bali. The Great Coral Reef. The Eiffel Tower, Statue of Liberty. Wake up Alice! Wake up! Alice! Alice! Alice!

Alice in deep sleep. Cheryl's voice mutates to Mother's.

13.

Voices singing, "Happy Birthday to Alice" and over this Mother's voice calling:

MOTHER　Alice! Alice! Alice! Where are you? What are you doing Alice? You'll be late for your own birthday! Everyone's waiting for you. There's cake! Put your new earrings on! We're wai... ting! Come down now! Alice?!

ALICE *(slowly coming to, calls out, disorientated, sleepy)* I... I'm coming!! I'm coming down!

MOTHER　What on earth has taken you this long? What have you been doing?

ALICE *(calling)* Nothing! I think I just fell asleep that's all! *(to herself. Puzzled. Dazed still)* Nothing. Just... getting ready... that's all... just getting ready...

Lights down.

The end.

Anna Furse

Is an award-winning director and writer. She has created over 50 performance works internationally – devised, text-based and multi-media. Artistic Directorships include *bloodgroup* in the 1980's and *Paines Plough* in the 1990's for whom she developed international co-productions and site-based works. In 2003 she founded *Athletes of the Heart* launching with *Yerma's Eggs* (Riverside Studios / Explore@Bristol). Other recent productions include: *Ultraviolet (DooCot), Kaspar - Speech Torture* (Cankarjev Dom, Slovenia), *The Peach Child* (The Little Angel Theatre / Japan Festival). Her play *Augustine (Big Hysteria)* has been produced in the UK, Denmark, The Czech Republic, Canada and the USA. *Gorgeous* toured the UK and Malaysia with Theatre Centre and was produced by the New Conservatory Theater, San Francisco in 2003.

She is Visiting Professor at Princeton University, USA and Lecturer at Goldsmiths College where she runs the MA in Performance.

Glow

Glow

When I was ten, me, my brother, my sister and our mates would make up plays and perform them. I especially remember doing a version of Michael Jackson's *Thriller* combined with *Tarzan*. This is how I got into Theatre.

– An Indian girl boxer who talks to Muhammad Ali. How did I get here?

I remember sitting on a bus when I was fourteen with my little sister. I heard: 'Paki bitches' from behind us. The abuse came from a white father and his son, who was about ten. Moments later, they started throwing lit matches. Deep inside, I wanted to go up to him and punch him, but I was afraid. Next stop, we got off the bus.

Kulwinder is a character who never stops fighting. On the exterior, it seems nothing can knock her, but inside she is dealing with all the confusions I had as a teenager. I chose Muhammad Ali to be her guide because he, like Kul in the play, never gives up – either in his sport or his life.

In *Glow*, I wanted to explore our parents as our heroes and what happens when we start to question them. The father throwing matches at my hair was still the little boy's role model.

My parents immigrated to England from India in the 1970's. A lot of their friends, like them, were great scholars and teachers who became bus drivers and factory workers. Unable to challenge their minds and live their dreams, our parents focused their energy on financial security and the education of us, the next generation.

At twelve, I was taken to an Anti-racist march. I remember being carried through the streets of London on my Dad's shoulders with hundreds of peaceful protesters, all nationalities, men and women. I saw my parents fighting to be heard in a land that didn't want to listen. *Glow* is a search for magic in an ordinary world.

Glow is dedicated to my father, Harbhajan Singh Virk and my mother, Jasvir Virk. Two of the many pioneers of their generation.

Manjinder Virk

Glow

Manjinder Virk

The play was first performed at Redbridge Drama Centre, London, 18th September, 2003. Directed by Dawn Walton, designed by Sophia Lovell Smith. Lighting designed by Ceri James.

KUL 14, British Asian girl, strong. **Nina Bhirangi**
ANT 14, Caucasian boy, slightly overweight. **Colin Kilbride**
RAJ Early 40's, Indian, Kul's father. **Anthony Mark Barrow**
ALI An essence of the boxer in his 30's. **Anthony Mark Barrow**
COMMENTATOR Colin Kilbride

Company Stage Manager / Production Manager – Marijke Zwart
Movement Director – Stephen Medlin
Composer – Duncan Chave
Accent Advice – Jan Haydn Rowles
Dramaturge – Noël Greig
Associate Artist – Paul J Medford
Casting – Bernadette O'Brien
Education Resources – Michael Judge
Production Assistant – Joseph Coelho
Set Builder – Set Up Scenery
Graphic Design – Iain Lanyon
Production Photography – Robert Day

With thanks to: Jo Balcombe and colleagues at Redbridge Drama Centre; Callum Dixon, Justin Pierre and Bindya Solanki for their work on the development of the script; teachers and students at Swanlea (E1) and Wanstead Schools in London.

Note: The action takes place over one week.

Possible Muhammad Ali quotes that can be used in the play:

"Silence is golden when you can't think of a good answer."
"If you even dream of beating me, you'd better wake up and apologise."
"It's just a job. Grass grows, birds fly, waves pound the sand. I just beat people up."
"The man who views the world at 50, the same as he did at 20, has wasted 30 years of his life."
"Float like a butterfly, Sting like a bee, your hands can't hit what your eyes can't see."
"If you suggest failure to yourself, you'll be a failure. Be the greatest."

SCENE 1

The stage resembles a boxing ring. We see a TV, a punch bag, a jar with money and a garland or framed photo of Kul's late mother in Raj's house. There are posters or images of Muhammad Ali in Kul's bedroom.
Muhammad Ali enters, dances on his feet and exits. Ali commentary could be heard from his 'Rumble in the Jungle' fight.
Kulwinder enters her gym. She works out. She starts the scene practising punches.
Antony enters. He is in a cinema queue. He is reading 'Lord of the Rings - Fellowship of the Ring' to the other people in the queue. (Throughout the play, Ant is munching on junk food.)

They speak simultaneously.

ANT *(reads)*	'One...'/
KUL	One.../
ANT	'Ring to rule them all'/
KUL	Two.../
ANT	'One...'/
KUL	One.../

ANT	'Ring to find them'/
KUL	Two.../
ANT	'One...'/
KUL	One.../
ANT	'Ring to bring them all'/
KUL	Two.../
ANT	'...and in the darkness bind them.'/ 'Three...'
KUL	Three.../
ANT	Rings for the Elven-kings under the sky/
KUL	Four, five, six.../
ANT	'Seven...'/
KUL	Seven, eight.../
ANT	'...for the Dwarf-lords in their halls of stone'/
	'Nine...'/
KUL	Nine, ten.../
ANT	'...for Mortal Men doomed to die!'

Kul continues boxing/warming up.
Ant shuts the book.

| ANT | I can't wait to see it! |

He looks in front of him in the cinema.

| ANT | What!? *'Lord of the Rings'* – Sold Out. No! |

SCENE 2
Kul's bedroom. Ant eats crisps.

KUL	Did you go?
ANT	Where?
KUL	Where do you think?
ANT	Sold out... *(mumbles)*
KUL	What? I can't hear you. Mumbler.

ANT   I ain't mumbling.

KUL   You are!

ANT   S-o-l-d o-u-t.

KUL   Didn't I tell you, it'd be sold out.

ANT   Didn't think it would.

KUL   You shoulda gotta ticket before. Everyone goes to
the pictures in half-term. I told ya.

ANT   Didn't have any money.

KUL   Should've got it off your Mum.

ANT   She didn't have any.

KUL   Your Dad then – he's loaded.

ANT   He's away working.

KUL   You shoulda nicked it off your brother then.

ANT   No, yeah, no, I did that before – he ain't got any.

KUL   You got the money now, ain't ya? Get a ticket for
tomorrow.

ANT   Spent it.

KUL   What on?

ANT   Stuff…

KUL   Crisps and crap, I bet.

ANT   Nah.

KUL   Yeah, where do you get them from?

ANT   I bought 'em. So what? It's my money I can do what
I like.

KUL   You can do what you like but you can't go to the
pictures. Cheese breath.

ANT   I ain't got cheese breath.

KUL   Phoar. Smells like my Dad's socks.

Ant opens his gob wide, showing the crisps.

KUL   Aww Ant, close your gob!
(Ant breathes on her.) Get lost! Give us a crisp.

(Ant takes one out and chucks it at her.)
Uggh, I ain't having that!

ANT	That's all your gettin'.
KUL	I think I deserve another.
ANT	Buy your own.
KUL	You should give me the whole packet.
ANT	Why?
KUL	Because I'm such a good boxer.
ANT	Yeah and really modest.
KUL	Give us it then.
ANT	Take *one* then.

Ant offers her the packet.

KUL   Alright, tight arse!
(She grabs the packet and starts shoving crisps in her gob.)
I need to eat as much as I can.

Ant takes out another packet of crisps from his pocket. He smirks.

ANT   Ah! You can have 'em. I got my own.

Kul and Ant sit eating crisps.

KUL   I'll remember this moment.
ANT   What moment?
KUL   The moment I had my first packet of crisps knowing
I was gonna be a champion like Muhammad Ali! *(Beat)*
ANT   Kul, you owe me a fiver.
KUL   What?
ANT   Have you got it?
KUL   What you on about?
ANT   You owe me a fiver.
KUL   So?

ANT   So – have you got it?

KUL   What?

ANT   The *fiver*.

KUL   No, I ain't got it.

ANT   But I need it so I can get my ticket.

KUL   You going to the pictures now?

ANT   Yeah, well, no.

KUL   So you don't need it now.

ANT   Oh Kul.

KUL   *Oh Kul.*

ANT   You're so full of it.

KUL   Ant, I was having a moment with my crisps where I was celebrating and you ruin it.

ANT   What you celebrating?

KUL   I told ya. You're looking at a champion.

ANT   You got through to the semi-finals!

KUL   Fights on Saturday. Gotta train every day this week.

ANT   That's really good. Why didn't you tell me before? What your Dad say?

KUL   Tell him later. If I win, I get into the championships next month.

ANT   Be back at school by then.

KUL   Don't remind me. *(Beat)*

ANT   So, Kul... does that mean you haven't got it?

KUL   What?

ANT   My money.

KUL   You want a fight about it?

ANT   Don't start.

KUL   C'mon, c'mon then.

Kul starts giving him play punches, winding him up.

ANT   *Oh, Kul,* leave us.

They have a mock fight but Kul punches Ant hard.

ANT   Ow! You gave us a dead arm.

KUL   You still want your fiver?

ANT   I'm going home.

KUL   I'm doing you a favour. If I give it to you, you'll
spend it all on crisps and *Curly Wurlys.*

ANT   I hate *Curly Wurlys* – they pulled out my filling
remember?

KUL   *Mars* bars then.

ANT   Don't eat them, either.

KUL   Whatever. When I win, I'll get you a box of crisps...
And some mouthwash.

ANT   I'm going.

KUL   Why?

ANT   Have to look after my brother.

KUL   See ya, then.

ANT   You gonna see me out?

KUL   Nah, you can see yourself out.

Ant goes home and sits in front of the TV.

SCENE 3
Raj in his living room. He is talking on the phone.

RAJ   I got the letter this morning... Mr Dillon... Dillon,
D-I-double L-O-N... The letter I got today is dated from the last
month... How can I pay you on time when I do not get the letters
on time? Eh? You have put on another one hundred pounds'
interest because I did not get the letter! ...Your loan offered
freedom from debts. What kind of freedom is that?
(Kul enters, she hears the end of the conversation.)
Check your records and sort out your mistakes. You cannot
expect people to come up with money like that!

He puts the phone down.

KUL	What's happened?
RAJ	Don't creep and crawl in like that.
KUL	I didn't. *(Beat)* How did it go today?
RAJ	What?
KUL	Didn't you have a job interview?
RAJ	Sit down, beti. I'll make dinner tonight. Shall I go to the chippy? We can eat fish and chips.
KUL	You got the job!
RAJ	Stop asking me questions Kulwinder!
KUL	But Dad...
RAJ	Do not ask about things you don't understand. It makes no difference if I go or not. They don't want someone like me. Nothing I do is good enough.
KUL	But you don't know, if you don't go.
RAJ	You think I should be a security guard? Working at *Kwik Save*? In the day, I can buy the food there and at night I can look after the food. I am not going for the jobs they hand out at the job centre. I am more qualified than the people behind the desks, who give me the paper to sign on. No, I need to be at home for you. Do you want me to work nights and never be at home like Antony's Mum and Dad? *(Beat)* Do you?
KUL	No.
RAJ	Run to the chippy. There's money in the jar.
KUL	They're savings...
RAJ	It's my money. I can spend it on what I like. We'll have fish and chips tonight.

Raj exits. Kul gets money out of the jar and exits.

SCENE 4

Kul is in the gym. We see her working out. Ali enters chanting, 'I may be poor but I am somebody, I may be poor but I am somebody.' He wears a robe. Ali is the embodiment of everything Raj was when he was young, when he had hope, self-belief and confidence. There should be a clarity when the actor changes from Raj to Ali, in the energy and accent. When he is Ali, he has a strong iconic presence. Kul talks to him.

ALI   Know where you're going and know the truth. Don't be what you don't have to be.

KUL   I'm in the semi-finals! Can you believe it?

ALI   You can get anything you work for.

KUL   Me! The only girl. Coach says I've gotta keep training.

ALI   You gotta do the work to be a winner.

KUL   I wanted to tell Dad.

ALI   Talk when you're ready to talk.

KUL   Two hundred and fifty quid, if I win.

ALI   It's the quickest way I could make money.

KUL   It's the quickest way I'm gonna make it. Give Ant a tenner and give Dad the rest to save up.

ALI   Stay focused.

KUL   He can get a suit so he can go to an interview looking smart. We can have fish and chips all week. *(Beat)* Do you think I can win?

ALI   You can do anything you want.

KUL   I'm gonna be one of the greatest.

ALI   To be the greatest you gotta act like the greatest and you know what – we all got it in us to be great.

KUL   I hope so.

ALI   You may be small but your actions can be big. Remember Rosa Parks? A black woman, who changed the law in America, because of her one small act.

KUL   She started a riot.

ALI   Blacks at the back, whites at the front. She wouldn't give up her seat for a white passenger because she knew she had a right to the seat as much as anybody else.

KUL   Yeah!

ALI	That led to the riot, that led to the change.
KUL	So the only chance you got to get anywhere is to fight.

Ali exits.

SCENE 5

Ant's living room. Ant and Kul watch TV. The sound of 'Popstars'/ 'Pop Idol'. Someone is singing Christina Aguilera's 'Beautiful'.

ANT	Oh my god, it's Tracey Ramsey.
KUL	What?
ANT	Oh my god, it's Tracey Ramsey!
KUL	No.
ANT	Oh my god! It's Tracey Ramsey!
KUL	Alright! I heard you the first time.
ANT	She's on telly, Kul!
KUL	What's she wearing? She looks a right slapper!
ANT	They're showing her for ages. Look at her. I can't believe we go to school with her and she's on telly! Look at her!
KUL	Alright, don't give yourself a heart attack.
ANT	Hope she gets through.
KUL	No chance.
ANT	I can't believe it!
KUL	Calm down! You're doing my head in!
ANT	She looked really good, don't you think? Not like Christina Aguilera, but she can sing an' that.
KUL	Don't tell me you fancy her.
ANT	No, I didn't say that.
KUL	You fancy her.
ANT	No.
KUL	Yes. She's got crabs.
ANT	Has she?
KUL	Yeah...

ANT	What are crabs?
KUL	Wait till I see her at school. I'm gonna well take the piss.
ANT	But she was really good.
KUL	You think Darius is good.
ANT	So?
KUL	Shame.
ANT	Someone we know was on the telly.
KUL	It's easy to get on the telly, everyone does it.
ANT	Who do you know who's done it?
KUL	My Dad's friend... he did something about – a documentary about – you know, getting his house done and that.
ANT	What? Like '*Home Improvements*'?
KUL	Yeah, that's the one.
ANT	I'd go on telly.
KUL	Who wants to see you on the telly?
ANT	Who wants to see you?
KUL	I never said I wanted to be on telly but I've got no choice but to live with it cos when I make it everyone's gonna wanna know me.
ANT	Yeah, sure.
KUL	I'll have em knocking my door down. I'll have to move somewhere far away so they don't know where I live, like the countryside or abroad. Like Posh and Becks. It'd be great. I'd have my own gym, won't have to go to school. I'd have money so I can do what I like. I can't wait. Don't look at me like that. You're lucky you got me as a mate.
ANT	I'm gonna get on telly.
KUL	Yeah – *Telly Tubbies*.
ANT	Ha ha.
KUL	You gotta do something to get on telly. You can't just be on telly for the sake of it.
ANT	Why not? Everyone else does it. Tracey Ramsey did it.
KUL	Did she win?

ANT   Dunno yet.

KUL   What's the point if you don't win? *(Beat)*
So what do you wanna do, Ant?

ANT   Dunno.

KUL   Not now – I mean what do you wanna *be*?

ANT   Dunno.

KUL   Dunno, dunno.

ANT   Why do you wanna know?

KUL   You jus' wanna get on telly?

ANT   I don't wanna.

KUL   But you said you did.

ANT   So?

KUL   You should learn to fight.

ANT   I'm alright.

KUL   I'll teach you some moves.

ANT   Nah...

KUL   I ain't always gonna be there to fight your battles.

ANT   I never ask you to.

KUL   You think I'm just gonna watch you get beat up.
That time I saw you in the corridor when Dunks was trying to
take your bag. If I didn't see him he would've laid into you, him
and Calvin. And that time Kirsty and that lot started shouting,
'Cheesebreath...'

ANT   Alright, alright Kul!

KUL   No one messes with me at school.

ANT   Dunks and that lot call you names as well.

KUL   What have you heard them say?

ANT   It doesn't matter.

KUL   What?

ANT   They're just... *(Beat)*

KUL   Say it.

ANT   They're just racist, aren't they?

KUL   They wouldn't dare say anything to my face. You
should learn to fight – you'll be alright then.

ANT   I want to be a hobbit. *(Beat)*
KUL   What?
ANT   Nothing.
KUL   You wanna be a hobbit?
ANT   Or a superhero.
KUL   You could be a hobbit, short arse.
ANT   It's like I disappear when I'm watching films. I'm in
another world.
KUL   On another planet more like.
ANT   When I watch the telly I'm gone, I'm with Pat
Butcher in the Queen Vic, with Vera Duckworth in *'Corrie'* but
then Mum shouts to tell me my tea's ready and I know it's not
real. The only time I really disappear is when I'm at the pictures,
that's when I'm really gone. In another world with action heroes,
superheroes, hobbits and wizards and anything that isn't me. In
'Lord of the Rings', I was Frodo looking for peace and freedom
for Middle Earth while under attack from the dark forces. 'One
ring to rule them all'. I can be a hero. I love it – falling, riding,
running, laughing, fighting – fighting with swords, fists, guns,
fighting wars and adventures that go on forever, always getting
the girl, having special powers, like going back in time or turning
into a bird and flying, flying through the skies like Superman or
jumping from buildings like Spiderman. It's magic and I love it,
complete magic.
KUL   Yeah, well, it's not the same in real life. Life ain't
got magic.

SCENE 6
Ant continues watching TV. Kul and Raj are in their living room.

RAJ   You got through?
KUL   Coach says I'm really quick on my feet. He says if I
keep working hard, I've got a chance at winning the championships. *(Beat)* But you don't have to worry about the training
money. I been saving my pocket money.

RAJ   Kulwinder I don't want you to put so much time into
boxing – it's not right. Use it for self-defence but you have to
think about your studies when you get back to school.

KUL   I don't want to do anything else.

RAJ   I was Number One in my class at all sports. I was
winning every competition when I was fifteen, in running,
cricket, wrestling. I was Number One.

KUL   I know Dad.

RAJ   My teacher said I can be a champion, a world
champion and I believed her. I came to England with the same
hopes, I started boxing. I was good. Even Muhammad Ali said it
when I met him.

KUL   I know – he shook your hand...

RAJ   He shook my hand and said I was in good shape. I
was in good shape. Even though I was an amateur, I was fit
enough to be a professional.

KUL   Dad –

RAJ   Things don't happen the way we want them to. This
world is not designed to help our people, understand? We made
this country a success, they made us failures.

KUL   You're not a failure.

RAJ   Look at you, Kulwinder. You look like a boy. You
think your mother would be happy if she saw you? It would break
her heart. You want to get married one day, don't you?

KUL   No, Dad, I don't.

RAJ   You want to be alone all your life? Knowing there is
someone you can grow old with is better than winning any
competitions. When that is taken away, what is left?

SCENE 7

In the street where Ant and Kul live. Ant pretends to be a Media
Commentator.

ANT   All the way from St George's Road, our very own,
home grown –

KUL   In yer face –

ANT	The unstoppable –
KUL	Three times world champion!
ANT	Five times world champion! The only girl to beat a man's record. The only girl to play a man's game as great as a man!
KUL	I ain't never been beaten.
ANT	She's never been beaten. She's a winner. She's a god.
KUL	Goddess!
ANT	A champ of all champs! Be afraid, like LL Cool J said, 'Mama's gonna knock you out.'
KUL	'I'm gonna knock you out, Mama said, knock you out...'
ANT	This girl is gonna knock you out.
KUL	You've seen the King now meet the Queen...
ANT	Kulwinder Dillon!
KUL	I'm changing my name, like Ali did.
ANT	But it's your name.
KUL	And I'm changing it. Like Ali did.
ANT	I could change my name too.
KUL	Why?
ANT	Dunno, could be someone else
KUL	You could change it to Cheesy.
ANT	Get lost.
KUL	Mr Cheese.
ANT	You think you can win?
KUL	Coach thinks I can.
ANT	Bet your Mum'd be proud.
KUL	Maybe...
ANT	Do you miss her? I miss my Mum.
KUL	What you on about? You ain't lost your Mum!
ANT	Yeah... I know, but I never see her, she's always working ain't she? Do you think about her?
KUL	Who?

ANT	Your Mum?
KUL	Can't remember her.
ANT	How can you forget her?
KUL	I ain't forgotten her.
ANT	But you said…
KUL	What about Katrina?
ANT	Katrina?
KUL	Queen of the Ring – Katrina!
ANT	Not sure…
KUL	What about Konny?
ANT	Queen Konny?
KUL	You think of something better.
ANT	How about… Kulwinder Dillon!
KUL	Be serious.
ANT	I am.

It starts raining.

KUL	Oh crap!
ANT	Take my jacket.
KUL	Why?
ANT	Cos it's raining.
KUL	You sure?
ANT	You don't wanna catch a cold before the fight.
KUL	Thanks Ant. Give it back tomorrow.

Kul leaves Ant. He shouts after her.

| ANT | See ya, Katrina! |

SCENE 8

Ant sits in front of the TV. He starts eating crisps. Kul is in her bedroom. Ali is with her.

KUL   Do you think I look more like a boy than a girl?

ALI   You have to see your own beauty.

KUL   What do you think Ant thinks?

ALI   Friends don't care about what you look like.

KUL   I can't believe he thinks Tracey Ramsey's alright.

ALI   Be your own person.

KUL   She's not all that.

ALI   No one sees you the way you do. *(Beat)*

KUL   No one's gonna go out with me, looking like this.

ALI   Appearances can be deceptive.

KUL   Dad said I'll be lucky if a peasant from India wants me.

ALI   The boxer Sonny Liston with his scarred face and slow speech was portrayed as a dumb jungle cat.

KUL   I don't want anyone to fancy me but I don't want them to think I'm a dog.

ALI   Sometimes we don't know how to say what we want. Then people think you are dumb. Sonny Liston wasn't dumb, he was inarticulate.

KUL   I don't know what I want.

ALI   We are all inarticulate when more has happened to us than we know how to express.

KUL   It's just not the same since Mum died. Dad doesn't want to talk to anyone. No one comes round anymore apart from Ant.

ALI   Sometimes the world we live in, doesn't make any sense.

KUL   Is he ashamed of me?

ALI   Living in a country that makes you feel like nothing.

KUL   He can't stand going out with me. Even when we go to *Tesco's*. I see him hiding his face so he ain't seen. In front of people who don't even know him.

ALI   Confusion. I prayed to a blonde-haired and blue-eyed Jesus but he weren't nothing like me. I was called a Negro

in my own country, allowed to go to some places and banned
from others because of the colour of my skin.

KUL   I'm the same as everybody else.

ALI   Why do people talk about not belonging? Who
decides? Is it God or man playing God? Home is where you
decide home is.

KUL   This is my home, this is where I was born.

ALI   Why do people call you 'paki'?

KUL   They don't.

ALI   The most powerful thing I did was get rid of my
slave name. I was Cassius Marcellus Clay and I became
Muhammad Ali.

Ali exits.

KUL   And I'm gonna be Katrina Dillon.

SCENE 9

*We see the three characters in the space. Kul boxing at the gym. Raj
sitting thinking, or on the phone at home. Ant watching TV and
eating at home. Kul gets a stomach pain and suddenly stops her
training. In a panic, she exits.*

SCENE 10

*Ant's living room. He is watching 'Lord of the Rings – The
Fellowship of the Rings' on DVD. Kul goes to Ant.*

ANT   What you doin' here?

KUL   Charming.

ANT   Why aren't you training?

KUL   Finished early.

ANT   But you can't finish early you got your fight on
Saturday!

KUL   I'm preserving my energy Cheesebreath. Here's
your jacket.

Kul and Ant sit in front of the TV. Pause.

KUL	Do I look different today?
ANT	What?
KUL	I dunno.
ANT	What have you done?
KUL	I haven't done anything.
ANT	What do you mean then?
KUL	Can you see anything different?
ANT	What you on about?
KUL	Do I look the same?
ANT	Yes, weirdo. *(Beat)*
KUL	What you watching?
ANT	'*Lord of the Rings.*'
KUL	But you've seen it.
ANT	I ain't seen this one.
KUL	Which one did you see?
ANT	The one at the pictures.
KUL	Ain't that the same?
ANT	No, this is the Special Edition DVD with an extra twenty-five minutes of the film that you don't see at the cinema.
KUL	Why not?
ANT	Cos they wouldn't have anything for the DVD then, would they?
KUL	You don't see the best bits unless you buy the DVD?
ANT	These aren't the best bits. They're just extra.
KUL	Extra rip off.
ANT	They're brilliant without the extra features but having extra features makes them even more brilliant. This bit's really good. See the black horses chasing her, well, they're the dark forces and she brings good to overpower 'em... The river turns into white horses... Frodo's ill – we think he might die.
KUL	Right. *(Beat)* When's your Mum back?
ANT	Why?

KUL	Wanted to ask her something.
ANT	You wanna talk to my Mum?
KUL	Yeah – so?
ANT	What do you wanna say to my Mum?
KUL	Nothing, forget it.
ANT	She said she had to do an extra shift at work. She'll

be back tonight. *(Beat)*

KUL	Am I your mate, Ant?
ANT	Yeah...
KUL	Your best mate?
ANT	I've known you the longest.
KUL	Can I tell you anything?
ANT	Yeah. *(Beat)*
KUL	Are you sure? It's really important
ANT	What is it?
KUL	Ant... I dunno how to say this.
ANT	Is it your Dad?
KUL	No, it's...
ANT	What's happened?
KUL	It's you! You've got a snot hanging off your nose!
ANT	Oh no, have I? *(wipes nose)* Has it gone?
KUL	Eghhh, you've wiped it across your face!

Ant tries to wipe it on Kul. They begin wiping it on each other, both are laughing.

KUL	Get off me! I was joking, you ain't really got a snot!
	Get off!!
ANT	You're in for it now!!

They play fight, she lets him win and he is on top of her. Ant quickly gets off her and starts watching TV.

ANT You gotta watch this, Kul. When I saw it the first time my favourite character was Frodo, who's a hobbit. Remember, I told you about him. Then I liked Gandalf but I've decided my favourite character is Sam now – Frodo's mate. Another Hobbit. He saves him. Even though Frodo has to look after the Ring, which is a big deal, if he didn't have Sam with him he'd turn evil and fall into the powers of the Ring – you get me? The Ring draws evil to it. It has to be destroyed, otherwise the Dark Lord will get a hold of it and he'll enslave the world. But cos Sam isn't affected by the Ring he keeps Frodo on track. *(Beat)*

KUL Ant, close your eyes.

Kul takes Ant's hand and places it between her legs. Ant quickly moves it away.

ANT *What you doing?*
KUL Nothing! I just…
ANT What?
KUL Did it feel warm?
ANT I don't know what you mean!
KUL I wasn't trying it on with you.
ANT Think you'd better go home.

Kul exits. Ant continues watching 'Lord of the Rings'.
Pause.

ANT Don't die Frodo. You won't. Your mates are there. Even the smallest person can change the course of the future. *(Beat)* Not if you're ugly, eh Frodo? Gotta be perfect to change the world. Sam's not perfect. It's horrible, Frodo. My body's horrible.

SCENE 11
Raj is in his living room. Kul enters.

RAJ	Have you seen the money in the jar?
KUL	What money?
RAJ	There should be ten pounds in the jar. I put ten pounds in there.
KUL	Dad, there wasn't ten pounds in there.
RAJ	How much was in there?
KUL	I don't know. I didn't count it.
RAJ	Did you spend some of the money? *(Beat)*
KUL	I have to buy something.
RAJ	How much did you take? *(Beat)*
KUL	Two quid.
RAJ	When is the training going to stop, Kulwinder?
KUL	It wasn't for the training.
RAJ	What did you need it for?
KUL	Nothing.
RAJ	What was it?
KUL	Nothing.
RAJ	Is that what you're spending all my money on? Boxing? How much?
KUL	Dad...
RAJ	How much?
KUL	I don't need the money for training!
RAJ	What do you need it for?
KUL	Here, take it Dad! Here's your two quid!

Kul gets two pounds out of her pocket and throws it at Dad and storms off to her bedroom.

SCENE 12

Kul's bedroom. She observes her body. Raj changes to Ali and enters her room. Ant watches TV.

KUL   Can you still box if you've started your periods? Think I started today. Thought it'd be red – more like brown sauce than tomato ketchup. It was really embarrassing. It was in the middle of my training. Don't know if the boys saw anything. I went to the loo and saw a brown splodge on my pants. Had to stop my training. I never stop. *(Beat)* I was stupid to think Ant'd know what to do. *(Beat)* Stuck some loo roll down there. Gotta get some pads. Don't wanna use *Tampax*. Don't know how. Have to use my training money, but I can't miss training. I gotta win.

Kul starts working out.

ALI   It's the quickest way to make it. Maybe the only way.

KUL   I will win.

ALI   I was no good at school. I had to find something else.

KUL   This is my only chance.

ALI   You only get one chance.

KUL   That's what Eminem said.

ALI   That's what I believe.

KUL   That's what I'm gonna do.

ALI   Who wants to be like those kids hangin' on the streets with nothing to do.

KUL   My Dad's lucky I ain't smoking weed and getting pissed.

ALI   I had nothing till I found boxing.

KUL   It beats everything. The buzz, the sparring, eyeing the opponent, a slap, punch and a clout.

ALI   A cuff and a wallop, to the left –

KUL   To the right and to the floor, not me but my opponent. Knockout!

ALI   King of the World.

KUL   I love watching you fight but I only get this feeling when I'm fighting, not watching – that's different, you can watch your whole life away. Watching everything, doing nothing.

ALI   Why does a man go to the moon? I say, because it's there.

KUL   Dad used to say I can do anything but I look at him
     and what's he doing?

ALI   Why did those blind people climb up that mountain?
     Because it was there.

KUL   And Ant just sits in front of the telly.

ALI   Why am I fighting for the title for the fourth time?
     Because it's there.

KUL   People on telly live their life to the full. They ain't
     watching our boring lives.

ALI   No man but me has ever won the title three times.

KUL   No girl but me has got through to the semi's. *(Beat)*

Ali exits.

KUL   But I'm not a girl now. I'm becoming a woman – no
     one knows.

SCENE 13

*Kul and Raj are sitting together in their living room. Ant is sat
reading 'The Fellowship of the Ring.'*

RAJ   Where is Antony?

KUL   Dunno. *(Beat)*

RAJ   Have you two had a fight?

KUL   No.

RAJ   Is he looking after his brother?

KUL   Dunno. *(Beat)*

RAJ   It has been a long time since we both sat together.
     (Beat)

KUL   Dad, did you go to school with Mum?

RAJ   What?

KUL   Were you at the same school as Mum?

RAJ   Hers was in the next village.

KUL   Do you remember when you first talked to her? How
     old were you both?

RAJ	It was a long time ago. *(Beat)*
KUL	I'm fighting in the semi's tomorrow.
RAJ	You are still fighting then.
KUL	I got you a ticket. It's a good seat. Coach said you'll be allowed to come to the dressing-room after. If you want to.
RAJ	I do not want to watch my daughter being hit.
KUL	I don't get hit.
RAJ	It is not right.
KUL	But Dad you got me into it.
RAJ	For self-defence.
KUL	Yeah and I use it for that as well.
RAJ	I want you to be safe.
KUL	I am safe. *(Beat)*
KUL	Mum watched every game you played at college, didn't she? *(Raj nods)* I can't believe Mum did that. I thought she hated sports.
RAJ	I don't know. *(Beat)*
KUL	What did she like doing?
RAJ	I can't remember.
KUL	She used to sing when she was cooking.
RAJ	Are you trying to upset me?
KUL	No...
RAJ	You have to torture me in this way just because I ask you not to box? You think I need reminding of my pain?
KUL	Sorry...
RAJ	I have enough to deal with. People sucking blood from me in every direction. Do you know how much money I am owing?
KUL	No.
RAJ	No you don't! How can you understand?

Raj exits. Pause.

KUL	I needed some money, Dad.

*Kul sits for a moment and then goes to the jar. She needs the money
for pads – she takes out two pounds.*

SCENE 14

Ant's living room. He watches 'Eastenders'.

ANT   Don't go home now! If you go home, you'll find
out! That'll be it. Divorce and then the trouble starts. Who's
gonna look after the kids? Maybe they won't get divorced.
They've been through a lot. She's lost a kid, he's had a car
accident, lost his memory and found it again. People get over hard
times. Mum and Dad don't even see each other but they're still
together. *(Beat)* They should be able to retire soon, amount of
work they do. Hate having to look after Jacob all the time. Little
brothers. Oh no! She's found 'em! Gutted. I knew that was gonna
happen. Always know what's gonna happen on '*Eastenders*'. It's
all happening. Broken hearts, falling out, making out, breakin' up.
(Beat) Wonder how Kul's doing. It's her finals tomorrow.

SCENE 15

*Kul is training in the gym. She is taking her frustrations out on her
punch bag. Ant enters.*

ANT   Alright Kul.
KUL   What do you want?
ANT   Ain't been to your gym before. *(Beat)* Went round
yours, no one answered.
KUL   I'm here ain't I? I'm not gonna answer the door from
here, am I?
ANT   Your Dad could've answered.
KUL   What do you want?
ANT   You ready for the fight?
KUL   You came all the way to ask me that?
ANT   No... Erm... I've come to get my fiver.
KUL   Right.
ANT   Have you got it? *(Beat)*

KUL   I've got your fiver ... But you ain't getting it.

ANT   When am I gonna get it?

KUL   Why don't you stick up for yourself Ant?

ANT   I do!

KUL   You'd get the crap beaten out of you if I weren't
with you.

ANT   No.

KUL   Yeah. What you gonna do if I don't give it to you?

ANT   Just give it us.

KUL   If you want the fiver. Get it off me.

ANT   What?

KUL   You want the fiver?

ANT   Forget it. I'm going.

Kul starts pushing him gently and it builds to her laying into him.

KUL   I'm talkin to you, Cheesey-breath. I said, get it off
me.

ANT   Leave us.

KUL   C'mon you're acting like a girl.

ANT   Jus' stop

KUL   Look at you, you're so scared. You can't even talk
back to a girl.

ANT   Leave it Kul.

KUL   *Leave it Kul, Leave it Kul.* I feel sorry for you.
C'mon, Stick up for yourself, Lard arse! C'mon, c'mon. Hit me
back!

ANT   Stop it Kul.

KUL   C'mon fatso, Hit me back, go on, I dare ya! Go on.
Who ate all the pies, Ant? C'MON, HIT ME BACK, LARD
ARSE!

*Ant loses it and pushes Kul to the floor and raises his wrist as if he is
about to punch her.*

ANT   DON'T! Don't... I HATE YOU! I HATE YOU!
You ain't my mate! I don't need you. I don't... Just leave me
alone.

Ant exits.

SCENE 16

*Raj looks around Kul's bedroom and finds the pads. He works out
that she has started her periods. Kul enters her bedroom.*

RAJ   Kulwinder.

KUL   What you doing in my room?

RAJ   Nothing. Is everything alright?

KUL   What do you want Dad?

RAJ   I want to talk to you, beti. Is that alright? Can a
father not ask that of his daughter? Since when did you become
so rude? *(Beat)* How are your holidays?

KUL   Why?

RAJ   Can you not answer a question any more? Do you
have to question everything I say? *(Beat)* Do you need to talk to
me about anything? *(Beat)*

KUL   No. *(Beat)*

RAJ   I know you... Er... need things.

KUL   I don't need anything.

RAJ   I will get you something tomorrow but I don't know
what size, and erm... I will ask at the Chemist.

KUL   Can you get out of my room?

RAJ   I went for that job you wanted me to go up for.

KUL   What job?

RAJ   The security guard. I went for an interview.

KUL   You did?

RAJ   They told me I did not have the right 'experience'.
To look after frozen food. *(Beat)* It means I have achieved
nothing.

Raj breaks down and starts crying.

KUL   Are you alright Dad? *(Beat)* Shall I make you a cup
  of tea? *(Beat)*
RAJ   I am trying, Kulwinder. *(Beat)* I am going for a
  walk.
KUL   Dad... *(Beat)* I could come with you.
RAJ   I need to be alone.

Raj exits.

SCENE 17
*Kul gets a sari out that is hidden in her bedroom. It is her late
mother's sari. She puts it on and then holds the material.*

KUL   Good night Mum.

She falls asleep in the sari.

SCENE 18
*Raj enters the living room with his old boxing gloves. He looks at
them – it has been years since he last saw them. He tries them on and
shadow boxes. He then takes them off.*
Raj stands outside Kul's room. He holds the gloves.

RAJ   Kulwinder? *(Beat)* Kulwinder, Can I come in?

Kul wakes up.

KUL   What?
RAJ   I have a surprise for you. Hurry up!

Kul leaves her room

KUL	What is it, Dad?
RAJ	What are you wearing?
KUL	I … Er...
RAJ	That's your mother's sari.
KUL	I know… I'm not supposed to...
RAJ	How dare you put her sari on! How dare you.
KUL	I just tried it on.
RAJ	Take it off. Never touch her belongings.
KUL	No.
RAJ	Take it off!
KUL	No, Dad!
RAJ	What are you doing to me?
KUL	I'm not doing anything, Dad. I just wanna be with

Mum. I don't wanna be with you, I just wanna be with Mum.

RAJ	Kulwinder…
KUL	But Mum's never coming back is she!
RAJ	Don't say that.
KUL	Cos she's dead, Dad. She's dead!

Kul storms out of the house.

RAJ   Kulwinder!

SCENE 19

Ant is sat reading 'The Fellowship of the Ring' out loud at home. There is a knock at Ant's door. It is Raj.

ANT	Oh morning, Mr Dillon.
RAJ	Hello Antony. Is Kulwinder with you?
ANT	No.
RAJ	She usually comes to your house.
ANT	It's her semi-finals today.
RAJ	I know.
ANT	She's probably gone straight to the gym.

RAJ   Yes, you are right. *(Beat)* What time are you going to the fight?

ANT   I'm... er... No, I don't think I can go.

RAJ   But she will be expecting you to be there.

ANT   I've... er... gotta look after Jacob, Mr Dillon.

RAJ   Oh. How is your brother?

ANT   He's fine.

RAJ   Does your mother have time to look after him?

ANT   I don't always have to look after him. Sometimes Mum puts him in the nursery.

RAJ   How is your mother?

ANT   Alright, I think.

RAJ   Your Dad is still away?

ANT   He's back on Tuesday. He's bringing the truck so me and Jacob can have a ride.

RAJ   You are lucky your father does special things for you.

ANT   Kul's the lucky one.

RAJ   She is?

ANT   Wish my Dad was at home all the time. *(Beat)* Say good luck to her from me.

RAJ   If I see her, I will tell her good luck.

Raj and Ant exit.

SCENE 20

Kul is in the dressing room of the gym. She starts warming up, getting ready for the fight. Ali enters. She still wears the sari.

KUL   How am I doing?

ALI   You gotta be strong to be a champ.

KUL   I've got to win.

ALI   It took me ten years to get my world title back, ten years!

KUL	I can't lose today.
ALI	They took away my world title because I refused to go to war in Vietnam to fight for freedom.
KUL	I'm fighting for what I want.
ALI	'Fight for freedom', they say. Whose freedom? I refused to fight for a country that didn't stick up for me at home.
KUL	I stick up for myself.
ALI	They weren't my opposers – they weren't my enemy – the people, in Viet Cong.
KUL	I've worked hard to get where I am.
ALI	The best fight I ever fought wasn't in America. I took the crowds to Zaire. *Rumble in the Jungle* with George Foreman!
KUL	I wanna be like you Ali.
ALI	Be your own person, not what somebody wants you to be.
KUL	You're the only person I look up to.
ALI	People you look up to may not be the people you want them to be. I looked up to Sugar Ray Robinson but when I first met him, he gave me no time of day!
KUL	I need someone to believe in me.
ALI	It's lack of faith that makes people afraid of meeting challenges and I believed in myself.
KUL	I can do it.
ALI	Champions aren't made in gyms. Champions are made from something they have deep inside them, a desire, a dream, a vision. They have to *glow*. The will must be stronger than the skill. *(Beat)*
KUL	Do you think I can win the championships?
ALI	Boxing isn't made for women.
KUL	It is.
ALI	They're not made to be punched.
KUL	I can take it!
ALI	They're not made to be beaten.
KUL	I believe in myself!

ALI   It's a man's sport.

KUL   I'm gonna win, aren't I?

ALI   What if you don't?

KUL   I will!

ALI   You know you can't do it, Kulwinder.

KUL   I'm not Kulwinder.

ALI   Kulwinder's your name, that's who you are. No
running away from that!

KUL   I'm Katrina.

ALI   Katrina is an English name, you're a paki.

KUL   I'm not!

ALI   That's what they call you at school behind your
back. Paki.

KUL   I'm not a paki.

ALI   Who are you then?

KUL   I don't know.

ALI   You're a woman.

KUL   I'm a boxer!

ALI   You're a woman and women shouldn't box! You
should be wearing skirts and acting like a proper lady, meeting
boys and thinking about babies, none of this boxing stuff.

KUL   I don't wanna be a woman!

ALI   Don't you wanna be like your mother?

KUL   She's not here anymore.

ALI   Have you forgotten your mother?

KUL   Don't talk about her!

ALI   She died in a car crash but that weren't your fault,
ain't your father's fault.

KUL   Stop it!

*Ali starts to take off her sari. Throughout the next speech she spirals
out of it.*

ALI   She's still your mother, you still remember how she
held you – her smell, her smile – but you don't wanna remember
because it's too hard and when life gets too hard, we wanna hide.
Run away from the pain!

KUL   Leave me alone!

ALI   Run away from the pain!

KUL   I said leave me alone! Go away!

Ali exits.

KUL   Ali? *(Beat)* Keep fighting, Kul. *(Beat)* Stay focused.

*Music. LL Cool J's 'Mama's gonna knock you out' plays. Kul enters
the boxing ring. A commentator is heard announcing the fight over
the speakers.*

COMMENTATOR Hello, ladies and gentlemen. Welcome to the
under sixteens lightweight semi-finals. You are here on a very
special day today, as we have, all the way from St George's Road
... our very own home grown-in yer face-the one-the only girl in
the fight....Miss KAAATTRINNNA DILLON!

*Kul stands ready to start the fight. A boxing movement sequence
follows with the commentary over the top. Raj enters from the
audience and sits down to watch the fight.*

COMMENTATOR No words have uttered from the girl who likes
to mouth off. What happened to that gob of hers? Can she walk
the walk or does she just talk the talk? Let's go straight to
ROUND ONE!!... She's checking her opponent but he's quicker
than she is. This girl fights like a girl. To the left, to the right, to
the left, left, right… and to her jaw!

Kul almost falls to the floor.

COMMENTATOR She's tough but not tough enough! She's taking a beating, she's taking the punches. To the left, to the right and…

Bell rings.

COMMENTATOR End of ROUND ONE!!

KUL To be the greatest you gotta act like the greatest. And we all got it in us to be great. *(Beat)* Even me.

COMMENTATOR ROUND TWO…! She isn't giving up. The girl's a fighter. She's giving as good as she's getting now. To the left, right, left, left, right. What speed! What grace! But no… What a blow! She's been knocked out! Oh, it's a shame but it's a game…

RAJ *(in Punjabi)* Thu carsac dee. You can do it, Beti. Thu thuckaree. [You can do it. You're strong, daughter.]

COMMENTATOR She's moving, She's back on her feet and back in the fight. To the left, to the right, left, left, right and… END OF ROUND TWO!!

Bell rings. Raj stands up and shouts.

RAJ Come on Beti! You can do it!

COMMENTATOR ROUND THREE!! She's back with full force. She's a dancer on her feet, a beauty to watch. A smooth punch to the left, uppercut to the right and … He's down! He's out cold! What a fight! The punch was good. Is he getting up? No! He ain't getting up! It's a knockout! We have a first time winner and the only girl to go through to the championships – MISSSS –

KUL Kulwinder Dillon.

SCENE 21

Kul and Raj are in the living room. Raj puts his hands together in front of the garlands as if he is finishing a prayer. Kul is holding her medal.

| RAJ | Your mother would never have believed you could |

RAJ   Your mother would never have believed you could fight like that. *(Beat)* I never believed it.

Raj gets out his old boxing gloves.

KUL   Are they yours?
RAJ   Yes. *(Beat)*
KUL   They look really old.
RAJ   I got them when I first came to England. I would sleep with them under the bed. I always thought they would bring me luck. *(Beat)* Put them under your bed.
KUL   Thanks. Where shall I put my medal?
RAJ   Don't you want to show it to Antony?
KUL   Oh... Yeah.
RAJ   He will be proud.
KUL   Maybe...
RAJ   I forgot to tell you, he said, 'Good luck.'

Raj exits.

SCENE 22

Ant is leaving his house. Kul goes up to him.

KUL   Ant! Where you going?
ANT   Kul. What do you want?
KUL   Erm... I just... thought you might wanna see my medal.
ANT   You won!
KUL   I told ya, I was gonna win.
ANT   That's really good. *(Beat)*
KUL   What you doing?
ANT   Gonna go and see 'Lord of the Rings'.
KUL   Again?
ANT   Yeah.

KUL	Who you going with?
ANT	I'm going with me, ain't I? *(Beat)*
KUL	Isn't your Dad back this week?
ANT	How do you know?
KUL	My Dad said.
ANT	Yeah. Tomorrow.
KUL	That's good.
ANT	Yeah. *(Beat)*
KUL	I got something for you.
ANT	What?
KUL	A tenner. Told you you'd get it back... with interest. Is it any good?
ANT	What?
KUL	The film?
ANT	I told ya. It's...
KUL	It's magic.
ANT	Yeah.
KUL	We'll see about that. What time is does it start?
ANT	Five-forty but they show loads of trailers so it probably won't start till six.
KUL	We got loads of time.
ANT	You taking that with you? *(Indicating her medal.)*
KUL	No you are.
ANT	What?
KUL	It's yours.
ANT	But you won it.
KUL	Yeah, but you're my lucky hobbit, ain't ya?

Kul gives the medal to Ant.

ANT	Thanks. *(Beat)* I'll come to the finals.
KUL	You better. *(Beat)* Come on then, I'm gonna get us one of those massive popcorn boxes and *Ben and Jerry's* ice cream.

Kul and Ant start walking down the road.

ANT   I don't eat *Ben and Jerry's.*
KUL   *Haagen Daz* then.
ANT   I only like the vanilla one.
KUL   Whatever. *(Beat)* Who's Frodo again?
ANT   Don't you listen to anything Kul? Frodo's the hobbit
that's gotta get rid of the ring before it gets to the dark forces.
KUL   And Sam's the best friend.
ANT   Yeah.

Lights fade.

The end.

Manjinder Virk

Writing credits include: *Leaving Turnpike Lane, Goodnight Butterfly* and *My Mood Today* (Royal Court Young Writers Programme), *Mr Sagoo lives at No.9* (Leicester Haymarket/Comedy Festival), *Forgive* (Kali Theatre Co.), *Tonight I Write* (BBC Radio 4).
Writer in Residence - Red Ladder Theatre Company (2002).
Acting credits include: *Ready when you are Mr Mcgill* (Working Title), *Unsuitable Girls* (Leicester Haymarket / Pilot Theatre Company), *Workers Writes* (Royal Court), *Midsummer Night's Dream* (Belgrade Theatre), *Trial by Jury* (BBC), *Millennium Mysteries* (Teatro Biuro Podrozy / Belgrade Theatre).
Artistic Director of Pangran Dance Theatre (1995-98)
Choreographed: *Tanz* (International tour), *Exploration of Loss* (Dance Festivals, UK), *Fear of Glass* (Arts Alive Festival).

Souls

Souls

For the Windrush generation

"Thank you so much for making that journey,
we love you."

For my generation

"Keep blazing the trail people"

For the next generation

"Know yourself, be yourself, love yourself"

*Dedicated to my family, whom I love so much
but never say it enough.*

Peace

Roy Williams

Souls

Roy Williams

First performed on 5th October 1999, at Highbury Grove School, London N5 and later given an enhanced production and tour in 2001. Directed by Michael Buffong and designed by Sophia Lovell Smith. *Souls* was subsequently invited to the inaugural European Urban Theatre Festival in Holland, in December 2002.

STEPHEN	**Declan Wilson**
ALEX	**Clinton Blake**
ANTHONEY	**Andrew Fraser**

Company Stage Manager / Production Manager –Tim Hughes
ASM (Rehearsals) – Emma Barrow
Composer – Delroy Murray
Movement Director/Associate Artist – Lawrence Evans
Voice Consultant – Bernadette O'Brien
Education Resources – Brenda Murphy
Dramaturge – Bonnie Greer
Graphic Design – Iain Lanyon
Production Photography – Timothy Nunn

With thanks to: All the artists and students (from St Mary's School, Hendon) who helped with the research and development of *Souls*; Irma Inniss; Dennis Buckley for help with set construction; Jan Haydn Rowles for accent advice; Nottingham Roundabout for the loan of their van; the staff at Oval House Theatre, London.

SCENE 1

Living room. Stephen, dressed in black, comes in. He looks around the room slowly, picking up things from the cabinet, table, putting them back. He pauses for a moment, looking at his mother's favourite chair before sitting in it. He finds one of her yellow notes, he laughs as he reads it. The front door opens. Stephen hides in the other room. Alex, also in black, comes in. He gets a drink from the cabinet. He does not notice Stephen creeping up behind him. Stephen tickles him underneath the arms, he jumps.

ALEX   Stephen!

STEPHEN   Yer gettin round boy.

ALEX   Grow up. What yu doin sneakin round?

STEPHEN   I wasn't sneakin around.

ALEX   It wass yu I saw at the back of the church weren't it? Why didn't yu come in?

STEPHEN   Mum wouldn't want any trouble.

ALEX   Yeah but yu came.

STEPHEN   Course I came. Yu ain't lookin any prettier.

ALEX   I could say the same.

STEPHEN   Yu could.

ALEX   Is that a wrinkle?

STEPHEN   On this face? How's Debbie?

ALEX   Gone. Next question?

STEPHEN   Yu two finally split up?

ALEX   As good as.

STEPHEN   Always said yu were a fool, now I know. Letting a beautiful wife like that go.

ALEX   What yu mean by trouble?

STEPHEN   Yu know me.

ALEX   What yu done now?

STEPHEN   Nuttin.

ALEX   How long yu stayin?

STEPHEN   I juss arrive man.

ALEX   I don't want no grief.

STEPHEN	Thass why I didn't come into the service.
ALEX	Yu stayin for the wake?
STEPHEN	Maybe.
ALEX	Up to yu.
STEPHEN	Nuff people at the church, weren't it?
ALEX	It was Mum. They're all comin back here. Yu awright?
STEPHEN	Yeah.
ALEX	I dunno, yu seem a bit, different.
STEPHEN	I'm fine.
ALEX	For real Stephen.
STEPHEN	For real. Look, I'm juss gonna pop out for a bit yeah. Get sum cigarettes and that. Don't look at me like that.
ALEX	How do yu know I'm lookin at yer?
STEPHEN	I can feel yer eyes digging into the back of my head. I'm coming back.
ALEX	Cool.
STEPHEN	Oh man, juss gimme some time, will yer?
ALEX	Time for what? Wass up wid yer?
STEPHEN	I'm coming back.

Lights fade.

SCENE 2

Living room. Later that day. Alex comes from the kitchen, carrying a plate full of sandwiches which he places on the table. He then starts going through some papers he finds from the cabinet. Anthoney is putting away some of his mother's things. He is carrying a cardboard box which he drops.

ALEX	What yu doin?
ANTHONEY	Anytime it's gettin too much for yu Alex, yu juss let me know yeah?
ALEX	Boy love to moan.
ANTHONEY	Why we have to do this today?

ALEX   Mum said.
ANTHONEY I never hear her say it.

Alex reads from one of the many yellow stickers placed around the room.

ALEX   'Alex, mek sure yu pack away all of my tings after de funeral, nuh wait.'
ANTHONEY Yeah, 'Alex make sure,' not Alex make sure Anthoney does it. Bloody hell man.
ALEX *(reads from another sticker)* 'Anthoney! Do not swear.'
ANTHONEY Piss off.
ALEX *(reads another)* 'I mean it young man.'
ANTHONEY Yer dry, Alex.
ALEX   Ain't me little brother, it's Mum. *(shows him the sticker)*
ANTHONEY Yeah? Wass she gonna do, clout me round the head?

Alex eats one of the sandwiches, it tastes awful but he tries to hide the fact.

ANTHONEY How can yu eat that?
ALEX   It's awright.
ANTHONEY Yu lie man, they're nasty. Didn't yu notice no one was eatin dem? *(He eyes an old photo, he picks it up.)* Wass this?
ALEX   Hey!
ANTHONEY *(laughs)* Yu dat? Wid the mash up trousers.
ALEX   Anthoney!
ANTHONEY Yu waitin for the flood?
ALEX   Yu want a slap?
ANTHONEY Yellow definitely ain't yer colour, dread.
ALEX   They were fashionable once.
ANTHONEY *(laughs)* Now yu know yer lying.
ALEX   Ask Debbie.

ANTHONEY Deh were fashionable? Deh were criminal. And wass wid the hair please?

ALEX There's nuttin wrong wid my hair.

ANTHONEY Mr Afro. *(picks up another picture)* Who's that?

ALEX Wass the matter wid yu, yu don't recognize yer old man?

ANTHONEY Dat him?

ALEX Na it's a total stranger thass kissin up yer mudda.

ANTHONEY How was I supposed to know? Mum never kept that many pictures of him. He looks different in the other one.

ALEX What other one?

ANTHONEY One wid him by his car.

ALEX Gimme it.

ANTHONEY No.

ALEX Anthoney.

ANTHONEY One picture man, what difference is it gonna make.

ALEX *(reads from another sticker)* Remember what I told yu boys, don't...

ANTHONEY ...look back, not ever. She ain't here, she ain't gonna know.

ALEX It's what she wanted.

ANTHONEY She didn't know what she was sayin, and yu, goin along wid it, this is our family.

ALEX Is that a joke?

Front door bell rings.

ANTHONEY I'm keepin it.

ALEX We'll discuss it later.

ANTHONEY We ain't discussin nuttin.

Anthoney goes to answer the door.

ANTHONEY Stephen! Awright man

STEPHEN   Yu awright our kid?
ANTHONEY Hey, less of the kid.
STEPHEN   Or what?
ANTHONEY I bus yer head.
STEPHEN   Come!
ANTHONEY Oh yu want to see sum moves now?

Anthoney and Stephen come into the living room, sparring with each other playfully.

ALEX   So yu show up now?
STEPHEN *(clips Anthoney on the cheek)* Boy!
ANTHONEY *(clips him back)* Boy yerself.
STEPHEN   So how's life, little boy?
ANTHONEY I told yu nuh, less of the boy.

They scrap again playfully.

ALEX   Enuff.
ANTHONEY *(stops)* He's so moany.
STEPHEN   Well?
ANTHONEY Goin college, ennit?
STEPHEN   Yu go college? A lazy git like yu? How the hell did
anyone in this family wind up goin college, man? Ennit Alex.
ANTHONEY Mum made me go. Bloody hate it. Bit late yer nuh
Steve, we had the funeral man.
ALEX   He was there.
ANTHONEY I didn't see him. Yu didn't tell me.
ALEX   I'm tellin yu now.

Stephen leaps onto the couch. He makes himself comfortable, rests his legs on the arm of the couch, Alex picks up another one of Mum's notes.

STEPHEN　　Oh man I've missed this couch. Wake me up when the football's on , nice. Oh and Anthoney, two sugars please.

ALEX *(reads)* 'Stephen, take yer leg off the arm of the couch.'

STEPHEN　　Excuse me?

ANTHONEY　Mum. From the dead.

ALEX　　　　That ain't funny.

ANTHONEY　Yu see me laughing?

STEPHEN　　Her and her stupid notes.

ALEX *(reads)* 'Stephen Arthur Brookes did yu hear me?'

STEPHEN *(sits up)* Sorry, Mama.

ALEX　　　　She knows yu too well.

STEPHEN　　Yeah, Mum knew everything. So did the old bag die then?

ALEX　　　　Hey.

STEPHEN　　I've heard yu say worse, don't even bother wid that.

ALEX　　　　When yu ever hear me say that?

STEPHEN　　Never mind when I juss have.

ALEX　　　　I do mind.

STEPHEN　　Don't matter.

ALEX　　　　Time and place, now.

STEPHEN　　Don't matter.

ALEX　　　　Ca' it never happened.

STEPHEN　　Whatever.

ALEX　　　　Sod whatever, I never called her names.

STEPHEN　　Alex, the perfect boy.

ALEX　　　　I ain't yu.

ANTHONEY　Yu two love to fight, ennit?

ALEX　　　　Move.

Anthoney gets up from Mum's chair. Alex takes his place.

ANTHONEY　It was a stroke.

STEPHEN　　Like before?

ANTHONEY　It was a bad one.

STEPHEN   I thought she were tougher than that.

ANTHONEY It's bin comin for months though. She ain't bin the same since she was mugged.

STEPHEN   Mum got mugged?

ANTHONEY Yu didn't know?

STEPHEN   When?

ANTHONEY 'bout a year ago.

STEPHEN   Who did it?

ALEX   We dunno.

STEPHEN   What yu mean yu don't know?

ALEX   Police never caught the guy.

STEPHEN   So what did yu do?

ALEX   What could I do?

STEPHEN   Nuttin as usual.

ALEX   So where were yu?

STEPHEN   I was away.

ALEX   Why yu can't say prison?

ANTHONEY Rah, yu were in prison, Stephen?

ALEX *(to Anthoney)* Yu turn deaf?

ANTHONEY Thought as much.

STEPHEN   What happened then?

ANTHONEY She wouldn't go out.

STEPHEN   That old bag was the strongest woman I knew. 'member when I was gettin picked on by Mark Palmer, Alex? Mum went right up to his house, banged on his front door, tellin his Dad, a big guy – yu know Anthoney – bin inside for GBH... Mum pressed her finger against his forehead, tellin him to tell his boy to leave me alone. Whole street come out and watched. *(Beat)* If I find that guy, he's dead.

ALEX   Yu ain't gonna do nuttin.

STEPHEN   Watch me.

ALEX   How yu gonna find him? Yer angry yeah...

STEPHEN   Angry? It don't boder yu sum low-life hurt our Mum?

ALEX   Yu tryin to be funny?

STEPHEN	Mugged!
ANTHONEY	I knew yu were in prison.
STEPHEN	Shut up, man.
ALEX	Don't yell at him.
STEPHEN	I wasn't.
ANTHONEY	I only asked.
ALEX	Shut up.

ANTHONEY Mum wouldn't admit it, no matter how many times I asked her.

ALEX	Mum didn't want yu to know.
ANTHONEY	What yu do then?
ALEX	Anthoney?
ANTHONEY	Come on broth, why yu go prison?
STEPHEN	Cos I got caught.

ALEX *(picking up the plate of sandwiches, to Anthoney)* Yu want another sandwich?

ANTHONEY No, throw dem in the bin.

ALEX Hey mister, Debbie spent hours making these, least yu can do is eat one.

STEPHEN Gimme the plate. *(takes a bite, spits it out)* Oh man.

ANTHONEY *(laughing)* See Alex, ain't juss me man.

ALEX *(to Anthoney)* Well, if yer ain't gonna eat, do sum work, make a change ennit?

ANTHONEY	Listen right, I bin doin all the work till now.
STEPHEN	What work?
ANTHONEY	Clearin out Mum's stuff.
STEPHEN	Yu can't wait?
ALEX	It's what she wanted.

ANTHONEY Photos, clothes, like she hated her whole life. *(shows the photo of Dad.)* Won't even let me keep this.

ALEX	Yu didn't even know the guy.
ANTHONEY	He was still my Dad though.

Anthoney looks at Stephen, then at the photograph. He looks hard at Stephen again.

STEPHEN   Alex, why is this boy lookin at me like that?
ALEX   Anthoney, what yu doin?
ANTHONEY *(puts his finger between his lips and nose)* Stephen do that.
STEPHEN   Why?
ANTHONEY Dead ringer fer Dad man.
ALEX   Anthoney?
ANTHONEY I'm juss sayin, look if yu don't believe me, he's a dead ringer for Dad. Grow a moustache Stephen man, yu could be twins. *(Alex swipes it)* Giss it.
ALEX *(to Stephen)* Yu want it?
STEPHEN Don't bother me.
ANTHONEY *(under his breath)* Is Mum gonna know, she watchin us?
ALEX   Yu got summin to say, speak up.
STEPHEN   That'll be juss like her ennit Alex – watchin us.
ANTHONEY I wish she was.
ALEX   Look, no matter what kid, can't destroy the memory in here. *(pointing at his head)*
ANTHONEY I ain't a kid man, can yu stop shamin me.

Stephen eyes Alex putting something in his pocket.

STEPHEN   What was that?
ALEX   What?
STEPHEN   Yu juss put in yer pocket.
ALEX   I didn't put nuttin.
STEPHEN   I saw yer.
ANTHONEY And me.
ALEX   Yu didn't see nuttin.
ANTHONEY It looked like a book.

STEPHEN   Got summin to hide broth'?

ALEX   Yer the one who loves to hide.

STEPHEN *(swipes the book out of his pocket)* Well have a look see.

ALEX   Giss it.

STEPHEN   Mum's bank book, what yu doin wid this?

ANTHONEY   Any money? *(Stephen opens it)* Rah! Two grand!

ALEX *(to Stephen)* Don't look at me like that. Ain't what yu think.

STEPHEN   Which is what?

ALEX   That I was gonna take it. I've got enuff money, honest money. Why do I wanna nick Mum's for?

STEPHEN   Yeah why?

ALEX   Yu callin me a thief? I juss found it.

ANTHONEY   Well, now that yu've found it, what are we gonna do? How we gonna get the money out?

ALEX   Is that all yu care about?

ANTHONEY   No. But if it's deh. I'm gettin a new phone – mobile phone Stephen, smart one too.

ALEX   Yu show sum respect for yer mudda, right. 'bout yu buying a mobile phone!

ANTHONEY   Awright man.

ALEX   Awright nuttin. Nuttin bothers yu does it, Anthoney? Not a ting. I see yu all day, wid yer stupid jokes carrying on wid yer bad attitude.

STEPHEN   Alex?

ALEX   Shoulda seen him though Stephen man, he don't feel a thing. Boy got a heart of stone.

ANTHONEY   Yu don't know nuttin.

ALEX   My Mum wasted her time wid yu, thass what I know.

ANTHONEY *(shoves Alex)* Yu wanna die or summin!

ALEX   Lickle Rah!

STEPHEN   Awright guys, come, let's juss chill, yeah? Nice.

ANTHONEY   I ain't dissing Mum, right. It's not my fault. *(leaves)*

ALEX   See how the little wretch like chat back. *(Stephen shakes his head)* Yeah what, yu got summin to say?

STEPHEN   Can't yu see he misses her? I could see it in his eyes the minute I come in, dread.

ALEX   Oh I see, yu turn expert now, sorry brudda, and how long's it bin since yu were lass here, exactly?

STEPHEN   Fine yu go after 'im den. Gwan.

ALEX   How am I supposed to know if he won't say nuttin?

STEPHEN   He shouldn't have to.

ALEX   And I weren't gonna steal it, right. *(leaves)*

Stephen delves into the box and finds some old photos, which he looks at. He then finds the torn photograph of Dad in the bin. He stares hard at it. He puts his finger between his nose and top lip. Stephen puts the photo in his pocket.

SCENE 3

Living room. Next evening. Alex is on the pay phone. He is holding a drink in his other hand. Stephen enters from outside looking very sweaty and carrying a basketball. He quietly sings to himself as he heads for the bathroom.

ALEX   Why wass up wid Glen? Well, let me speak to him. What did I do? No I don't know what I did, what I do? Debbie, please, please what did I do? What? I'm not getting angry, I'm not. Well, if I am, it's cos yer mekin me angry. I'm trying to have a civil conversation wid yu, but yu don't wanna know, it's like yu made up yu made up yer mind it ain't gonna happen. Look juss put Glen on the phone now please, I'm gonna straighten this out now. No? What yu mean no? He's my kid too, yu nuh. Done enough awready ... oh man, this woman mek me die, yu nuh! She tell I done enough awready and I don't even know what I done! Wat did I do Debbie!

Stephen comes back in, still singing.

ALEX   What? What... speak up man. Debbie my money's runnin out, ring me back, ring me back...

STEPHEN   That Debbie?
ALEX   Yu got any money, pound coins or summin?
STEPHEN   Nope.
ALEX   Why the hell Mum had to get a phone like this for?
STEPHEN   Tell yer man, that brother of ours is fast. *(throws him the basketball)* Catch.
ALEX   Oh no.
STEPHEN   What?
ALEX   Shit!
STEPHEN   What?
ALEX   I promised Glen I'll watch him play basketball for his school today.
STEPHEN   Sure it was today?
ALEX   It was today.
STEPHEN   Debbie woulda said.
ALEX   No. Thass juss like her, yu nuh, wind me up , mek me feel bad. *(mumbling)* Workin all hours, every blasted day, what they want from me?
STEPHEN   What?
ALEX   What?
STEPHEN   What yu sayin?
ALEX   Nuttin. *(mumbles again)* Mum die, but nuh they don't care about that, don't care how 'bout I'm feeling, what they want me to say?
STEPHEN *(getting irritated)* Alex?
ALEX   What? Lemme alone nuh guy. *(mumbles again)* Sorry Debbie, sorry Glen, that my mama's death inconvenienced yu, it won't happen again nossir.
STEPHEN   Will yu stop mumbling.
ALEX   I ain't mumbling.
STEPHEN   Yu don't even know yer doin it. Mum used to do that, mumble all the time, I wanted to throw my shoe at her. Wass up wid yu?
ALEX   I've lost it.
STEPHEN   Yer mind?

ALEX	The garage.
STEPHEN	Yu've said that before.
ALEX	This is for real.
STEPHEN	What yu done now?
ALEX	It's not my fault.
STEPHEN	Never is.
ALEX	If that guy hadn't sued me...
STEPHEN	If yu fixed his car properly...

ALEX   I did! I was sixteen when I first started workin there,
Stevie – sixteen man. Dropped outta school, worked nine to nine.
Garage bought my first house, kept this place goin for Mum, for
all a yu. It's mine.

STEPHEN   Is that why yu were trying to teif Mum's money?

ALEX   I wasn't teifing it.

STEPHEN   Yer lie bad.

ALEX   I was gonna borrow it, thass all. I could paid off sum
of my debts wid it.

STEPHEN   Yu weren't even gonna tell us.

ALEX   Anthoney's got a job man, he don't need all that
money fer college.

STEPHEN   Yeah?

ALEX   Mum left that money for him. She gave me a letter,
I'm supposed go to the bank next week and sort it. And yu know
what he's gonna blow it on – stupid clothes and music, chasin gal,
a mobile phone! I got a wife and kid to feed.

STEPHEN   Ex-wife.

ALEX   Hey it's over when I say it is.

STEPHEN   Suppose thass means she'll be on the market soon,
ennit?

ALEX   Listen yu, all I want is respect, right? Who held this
family together when Dad topped himself? Yu all owe me.

STEPHEN   Families don't owe.

ALEX   Didn't even cross Mum's mind to gimme sum. She
weren't blind, she could see what I was going through, what was
happening to me, ennit Mama? Or is this another one of yer

lessons? *(Beat)* Every day I see her sitting in that chair man, talkin my ears off, going on and on about rubbish. When she was growin up... how she met Dad... nobody was listening, nobody cared, 'cept me, but she still talked.

STEPHEN   She was old.

Alex goes to the cabinet for another bottle. A yellow sticker is attached to the bottom of it.

ALEX *(reads)* 'Alexander, don't yu think yu have had enough to drink?' No Mama, I don't. *(to Stephen)* And yu stay away from Debbie. Yu think she go free it up for yu?

STEPHEN   Is that a challenge?

ALEX   Mek a move, an I bus yer head.

STEPHEN *(pretends to shudder)* Oooh!

ALEX   Tell me summin – how d 'yu do it? How d 'yu keep screwin things up fer yerself on a regular basis, breakin yer mother's heart whenever yu get a chance, and still have that smug smile on yer face?

STEPHEN *(grins)* Practice.

ALEX   Yer such a bad boy, don't mess wid Stephen Brookes, juss remember right, I used to change yer nappies when Mum was at work – yu think yer Dad wanted to do it? I never knew so much crap could come outta one shitty little behind – yu stank. There's nuttin yu can do to scare me.

STEPHEN   I know yu ain't scared of me.

ALEX   Damn right.

STEPHEN   Come on big guy, time for bed.

ALEX   Get yer hand off me.

STEPHEN   Ease up.

ALEX   Yer lucky I don't ease up all over yer face, mate.

STEPHEN   Fine, stay which part yu deh. *(Beat)*

ALEX   Stevie?

STEPHEN   Wat?

ALEX   Why didn't yu let anyone visit yu in prison?

STEPHEN	Where did that come from?
ALEX	Why? Yu let us visit las time, why not then?
STEPHEN	Go drown yer head.
ALEX	Maybe ca', yu weren't there.
STEPHEN	What yu talkin about – I weren't there?
ALEX	Time to come clean Stephen Arthur Brookes.
STEPHEN	I was there, right.

ALEX   Ain't what Robbie says. Yu remember yer mate Robbie, he was inside same time as yu – Scrubs right, he didn't see yu there, funny that.

STEPHEN   What yu doin – checkin up on me?

ALEX   I met him down the High Street this mornin' awright, he was askin after yer.

STEPHEN   What yu turn policeman now?

ALEX   See what I can't figure out is – is yu puttin Mum through all that agony, lettin her think yu were in prison, making Anthoney idolise his big bad brother... So where were yu?

STEPHEN   None of yer business.

ALEX   Yu see, I know there's summin yu ain't tellin us Stephen, I know. So come on, where were yu? Tell me, tell me, *(starts clipping him around the head)* Come on, come on, come on.

STEPHEN   Don't do that, don't do that, get off me. Yu think I'm still a kid, yu can slap me about.

ALEX	I hardly touched yu, yu lickle gal.
STEPHEN	Yu wanna know where I was?
ALEX	Yeah.
STEPHEN	Believe me broth', yu ain't ready to know. *(Pause)*
ALEX	I need money.
STEPHEN	How much?
ALEX	A lot of it. And I ain't no teif.
STEPHEN	What yu askin me for?
ALEX	I want yu to arrange an accident for me.
STEPHEN	What kind of an accident?
ALEX	Stephen don't play around, right.

STEPHEN   Well, say it den.

ALEX   The bloody garage, awright! I want yu to torch it. I
want yu to light it up, I want it burnt to the ground, so I can claim
back on the insurance, yu understand me now?

STEPHEN   Why yu come to me? Yu come straight to me wid
this.

ALEX   Ca' I know yu.

STEPHEN   Yu know me? Wass my favourite colour? Which
team do I follow? Who was my first gal?

ALEX   How much?

STEPHEN   Yer a scumbag, Alex. Yu were a scumbag when we
were kids...

ALEX   Stephen?

STEPHEN   And yer still a scumbag. *(Beat)*

ALEX   How much yu want?

STEPHEN   Five hundred.

Lights fade.

SCENE 4

*Living room. Stephen and Anthoney are playing together on
Anthoney's 'Playstation'.*

ANTHONEY Oh yes, suffer! Had enuff?

STEPHEN   Don't worry about me, juss gettin started.

ANTHONEY After fifteen goes? Who yu gonna be now?

STEPHEN   Yoshitmitsu. What yu laughin for?

ANTHONEY Soft.

STEPHEN   Watch me kick yer butt now.

*The brothers play. Stephen seems to be doing well, intially. But not
for long. Anthoney wins the game.*

ANTHONEY Suffer!

Stephen throws down his controller in defeat.

ANTHONEY Another?
STEPHEN I know when I'm beat.
ANTHONEY Soft, man.
STEPHEN Come outside wid the basketball again little man, I'll show yu who's soft. *(Anthoney carries on playing)* Yer good though.
ANTHONEY I know.
STEPHEN Where yu learn to play?
ANTHONEY I learnt myself.
STEPHEN Amazing what they can do, smart little box.
ANTHONEY Yeah.
STEPHEN Expensive, ain't they?
ANTHONEY Bit.
STEPHEN So where yu get it?
ANTHONEY Told yer, bought it off a mate.
STEPHEN Oh yeah. So who did he steal it from then, Anthoney?
ANTHONEY What yu chattin about – ain't nicked.
STEPHEN Come on broth'.
ANTHONEY It ain't.
STEPHEN Never lie to a liar. I've bin here a couple of days, ain't seen yu in years – ask yerself, how do I know it's nicked?
ANTHONEY Yu bin in my room?
STEPHEN CDs, Walkman, laptop, thass a serous bitta stash yu got stashed there brother.
ANTHONEY What yu doin goin in my room?
STEPHEN That used to be my room. I was havin a look round.
ANTHONEY Don't business yerself wid my business.
STEPHEN Anthoney if I see a big suspicious looking black bag, stickin out from behind the wardrobe, course I'm gonna look. Stupid place to hide, don't yu think?
ANTHONEY Where would yu have put it?

STEPHEN	Up in the loft. Mum never went up there.
ANTHONEY	Look I'm mindin them for a mate right.
STEPHEN	What mate?
ANTHONEY	Barry.
STEPHEN	Barry don't have a home of his own?
ANTHONEY	He lives wid his Mum and Dad still.
STEPHEN	Oh right, OK. Hand me the paper please, Anthoney.

(Anthoney gives him the newspaper) Cheers.

Stephen clouts him around the head with the paper.

ANTHONEY	Oi! Juss move right.
STEPHEN	Don't ever let people use yu.
ANTHONEY	I ain't.
STEPHEN	What if the police come in here now? What would they see? Yu playin on that – yu stupid?
ANTHONEY	No.
STEPHEN	Mr. College man.
ANTHONEY	So why yu play *Tekken* wid me if yu knew it was nicked?
STEPHEN	Curious to see how far yu take it.
ANTHONEY	Yu were crap anyway.
STEPHEN	Whatever.
ANTHONEY	Yer off yer head.
STEPHEN	Whatever.
ANTHONEY	'bout yu hittin me.
STEPHEN	Stop mumbling.
ANTHONEY	Take another pill.
STEPHEN	What?
ANTHONEY	Saw yu in the bathroom this mornin, takin sum pill.
STEPHEN	I had a headache.
ANTHONEY	Yeah right.
STEPHEN	Yu didn't see nuttin.
ANTHONEY	I saw yer.

Stephen grabs his brother by the collar.

STEPHEN   Yu didn't see a thing.

ANTHONEY Get off me. Yer lucky I don't fling myself at yu.

STEPHEN   Yu got a brain, use it.

ANTHONEY Yu don't know where I'm from. Come like Mum, come like Alex. They wanted me to go.

STEPHEN   That so bad?

ANTHONEY Yeah, cos I had it. Ain't gonna learn nuttin. I don't know what I'm doin there.

STEPHEN   So what yu gonna do out deh wid Barry? Yu think it was someone wid 'A' Levels who mugged our Mum?

ANTHONEY We ain't stupid.

STEPHEN   Yer gonna get nicked.

ANTHONEY Ain't happened yet.

STEPHEN   Ah, yu tink yer badman?

ANTHONEY Come outta my face. Yu turn dry now. Ca' true say I ain't hating my life like Mum, right, like Dad. The guy bottled it.

STEPHEN   He did what he could.

ANTHONEY He bottled it. Let himself get beat. I don't care if he did lose his job – don't give 'im the right to kill himself, Stephen, it don't. Shamin me. He was weak.

STEPHEN   What yu know what he was?

ANTHONEY I don't see him here.

STEPHEN   Listen yeah, not having a job might mean nuttin you yung'uns these days, but it meant a lot to yer old man, yeah. Are yu listening? Providing fer him family, takin care of dem.

ANTHONEY Yeah, till I come along.

STEPHEN   What yu say?

ANTHONEY Yu of all people I thought would understand. All dis time, I thought yu were the man.

STEPHEN   I'm thirty-four, thass what I am.

ANTHONEY Yer point?

STEPHEN   I'm thirty-four. And I got nuttin to show for it. Yu get me?

ANTHONEY *(lying)* Yeah.

STEPHEN   I look like a fool to yu? I was sittin where yu were once, listening to sum rubbish Mum was givin me about leadin an honest life – gave her the same look yer givin me now.

ANTHONEY Then yu know what I'm chattin about – yu can't handle I got it – yu ain't.

STEPHEN   What?

ANTHONEY The feelin, the buzz – yu had it, lost it, but yu want it back though – I can see it in yer eye, dread.

STEPHEN   Yu don't know what buzz is.

ANTHONEY Tell me, den.

Alex enters, looking stressed.

STEPHEN   Wass up broth'?

ALEX   That stupid dog from downstairs was chasin me again. Ugly little half-breed ting, it love chase people.

ANTHONEY Mum was the only person it didn't chase. Too 'fraid.

STEPHEN   Can't believe yer still scared of dogs, man.

ALEX   I ain't scared of them. They juss don't like me. Tellin yu, that old git lets it do it on purpose.

ANTHONEY Dash a brick at it, it get the message then.

ALEX   Hey, yungsta... why ain't yu at college?

ANTHONEY Study day.

ALEX   So go study, nuh?

ANTHONEY Guy love to mek up noise.

STEPHEN   Don't need go college do yer, Anthoney?

ANTHONEY Nope.

STEPHEN   What can he learn that he can't learn from his brothers?

ANTHONEY Ennit.

ALEX *(whispers)* I got the ting.

STEPHEN   What ting?

ALEX   The ting.

STEPHEN   Could yu be a little more specific?
ALEX   Anthoney, get me a coke.
ANTHONEY   Yu see dem two tings growin outta yer body – dem called legs.

Alex gives his brother a glare. Anthoney takes the hint and does as he is told. Alex hands his brother an envelope.

ALEX   It's all locked up. Padlocked. Shouldn't be a problem right? It's gotta look good, Stephen. Them insurance people ain't stupid, right. And I need that money, dread... tellin yu, I need it bad. *(Stephen takes out the money and starts counting.)* Wat yu doin?
STEPHEN   Wass it look like? No offence.
ALEX   Stephen?
STEPHEN   Shut up man, losin count.
ALEX   Anthoney's comin, put it away.
STEPHEN   What, he ain't seen money before?
ALEX   What yu playin at?
ANTHONEY   Here tek yer can yu lazy – rah man, wass wid the wad?
ALEX   Go to yer room.
ANTHONEY   How much yu got there?
STEPHEN   'bout five hundred.
ANTHONEY   Dash me a tenner.
ALEX   It's juss a loan.
STEPHEN   Now, now Alex, don't tell lies.
ANTHONEY   Wass it for?
STEPHEN   Little job yer brother wants doin.
ANTHONEY   What job?
ALEX   Don't –
STEPHEN   I left home when I was younger than him, Alex, or should I say – thrown out.
ANTHONEY   Wass the job, man?
STEPHEN   Answer him.

ALEX   Why yu doin this?

STEPHEN   He ain't as pure, as yer think.

ALEX   Meanin?

STEPHEN   Tell him.

ANTHONEY   I ain't going back to college.

ALEX   Since when?

ANTHONEY   Since always.

ALEX   Yu can't juss throw it all away.

ANTHONEY   Watch me.

ALEX   Yu selfish little runt.

ANTHONEY   Don't care.

ALEX   That was the only thing that kept Mum goin, yu nuh. To see yu do well fer yerself.

ANTHONEY   I didn't ask for it.

ALEX *(to Stephen)* What yu done to him?

STEPHEN *(playing the innocent)* Me?

ALEX   I've only bin gone a blasted hour.

ANTHONEY   So wass the job, broth'?

STEPHEN   Yu want come?

ALEX   No, he doesn't.

ANTHONEY   Tell me.

STEPHEN   Biggest buzz there is. Go upstairs and change first. Dark clothes, whatever yer got.

ALEX *(grabs Anthoney)* Sit down. *(Anthoney breaks free, goes upstairs)* Anthoney? *(To Stephen)* Yer sick. What kinda guy lets his brother do that?

STEPHEN   Yeah Alex, what kinda brother?

ALEX   Yer different.

STEPHEN   Am I?

ALEX   Yu think I go let him walk out?

STEPHEN   He's gone already broth'. Yer juss too blind.

ALEX   Wass the matter wid yu? I mean I always knew yu had a nasty streak in yer – but this. Where exactly yu bin all this time, Stephen? The nuthouse or summin?

STEPHEN   I think yu'll find they're called mental hospitals,
Alex.

ALEX   Gimme back my money.

STEPHEN   Deal's a deal.

ALEX   I'll get someone else.

STEPHEN   For five hundred? Yu really think thass the going
rate?

ALEX   This is juss my luck, ennit? The one person I go to
fer help/

STEPHEN   /I'm yer brother man!

ALEX   /is a basketcase.

STEPHEN   Tell Anthoney, I'll meet him outside.

ALEX   I'll call the police.

STEPHEN   Call them. Go on – call them. Yu'll go down as well.

ALEX   Leave now. Please Stephen, juss go.

STEPHEN   He wants to come.

ALEX   Don't mean he has to. I ain't gonna ask what
happened to yu, I don't wanna know. But there's gotta be a part
of yu – bitta Mum tellin yu it's wrong. *(Stephen laughs)* Yer evil,
Stephen.

STEPHEN   Look, right, it don't matter if he comes or not, I ain't
waiting around. *(He exits)*

Anthoney comes down, dressed in black.

ANTHONEY Where's he gone?

ALEX   Get back up and change.

ANTHONEY I'm goin wid him.

ALEX   Yer goin back to college.

ANTHONEY I ain't learnin nuttin deh.

ALEX   What yu gonna learn from him? Can't yu see, he's
sick in the head?

ANTHONEY Yer sick. What yu got him to do fer yer?

ALEX   Don't worry yerself.

ANTHONEY It's about all that money yu owe, ennit?

ALEX   How yu know that?

ANTHONEY   I live in this house as well, yu nuh. I used to hear yu and Mum. It's happenin again, ennit, juss like Dad.

ALEX   Calm down

ANTHONEY   If Stephen can help yu, let him. Let me. *(Beat)* I know yu hate me Alex.

ALEX   Shut up.

ANTHONEY   Yu do. Yu blame me for Dad.

ALEX   What?

ANTHONEY   Dad lost his job – I was on the way. He couldn't hack it. Yu blame me for being born.

ALEX   Nuh man, yer wrong.

ANTHONEY   Yer lying.

ALEX   How long yu bin feeling this?

ANTHONEY   All my life.

ALEX   Anthoney, yer wrong, listen to me...

ANTHONEY   No.

ALEX   Yu walk out that door.

ANTHONEY   Yu won't call the police. Yu know yu won't. Come wid us. So yu wanna end up like Dad, now?

ALEX   That ain't gonna happen to me. Don't even think that. Stephen is gone, yeah – he's on another planet. Don't let me lose yu as well. Go upstairs and change. Please, Anthoney.

Anthoney leaves. Alex walks around the room, cursing but it sounds more like mumbling. He then grabs his coat and goes after them.

SCENE 5

Living room. Stephen enters – he looks like hell. He runs into the bedroom ands comes back out with his clothes, which he stuffs into his bag. He is in a real panic. He jumps when the doorbell rings, but does not answer it. He remains still. The doorbell continues to ring. It stops. Stephen waits a few seconds before resuming to pack his clothes. He stops again, and looks around, like he can sense someone is there in the room.

STEPHEN   Mum?

He jumps again when the front door slams. Alex comes bursting in.

ALEX   What did the police want?
STEPHEN   I dunno, I weren't gonna open the door.
ALEX   Come here.
STEPHEN   What, so yu can hit me?
ALEX   Yu are stupid, yu got no brains.
STEPHEN   What yu moanin for?
ALEX   One little fire, thass all.
STEPHEN   It's what yu get.
ALEX   So why yu leave Anthoney behind?
STEPHEN   Yu were runnin too, Alex.
ALEX   He was wid yu.
STEPHEN   We got separated.
ALEX   I shouldn't have trusted yu.
STEPHEN   Yu blamin me?
ALEX   Yu shouldn't have left him. One little fire, thass all.
STEPHEN   Will yu stop sayin that, please.
ALEX   So what happened?
STEPHEN   I don't blasted know! Someone musta saw us break
in or summin, call the police on us.
ALEX   Didn't think of that, did yer?
STEPHEN   No, I guess not. Look, yu came to me, yu got what
yu wanted.
ALEX *(sees bag)* Wass this? Yu little git, yu were gonna run,
weren't yer?
STEPHEN   Yu tink I'm gonna stay here? Don't look at me like
that. What yu gonna do? Go to the police and put up yer hands?
That yu did it for the insurance? I dare yu. I'll pay money to see
that.
ALEX   Anthoney won't talk.

STEPHEN   He's soft man, course he's gonna talk. How long yu
think it's gonna take before they find out, he's our brother?

ALEX   He shouldn't have bin there.

STEPHEN   We're beyond that now.

ALEX   Man!

STEPHEN   Come wid me. I'll wait for yer, five minutes, go
pack yer bags. Come wid me.

ALEX   If yer Mama was here.

STEPHEN   Well, she ain't. She try to raise us right, didn't work
out, so what?

ALEX   We leave him behind.

STEPHEN   Mummy's little golden boy, yes.

ALEX   It's wrong.

STEPHEN   Yu can't go prison broth', yu don't wanna go there.
The police could be coming back right now, man.

ALEX   Yu go. I say it was yu.

STEPHEN   What?

ALEX   Ain't like they'll be surprised. I gotta son, man.

STEPHEN   Yu know what yu can do wid that idea. Yu bloody –
I got half a mind to stay right here and watch yu go down too, yu
nuh.

ALEX   Go Stephen – run like yu always do – yer good at it,
they won't find yu, juss go. Don't juss stand deh. *(Beat)* Fine,
stay which part yu deh. I don't know why I even listened to yu.
One fire. Yu can't do nuttin right, all yer life. Come juss like Dad.

Stephen goes for his brother but Alex fights back.

ALEX *(holds him down)* What did I say Stevie, yu don't scare me.
(Stephen breaks down in tears) What yu doing? Get off, get off,
get off me. What yu cryin for?

STEPHEN   Stevie Brookes don't cry... Stevie Brookes is a
wort'less teif.

ALEX   I ain't doin this.

STEPHEN   Scared?

ALEX   Yu carry on like yu me to look after yer again... Yu
ain't my little brother, no more. Shoulda thought about this
before, right, yu should have. How many times I watch Mum,
gettin all stressed, worry about what grief yu go give her next.

STEPHEN   Shoulda bin like yu, perfect son.

ALEX   I weren't perfect, I juss weren't yu.

STEPHEN   And yu never looked after me, yu used to bully me.

ALEX   Yu best go now.

STEPHEN   No.

ALEX   Tek care of yerself, Stevie.

STEPHEN   Yu deaf?

ALEX   Awright, stay then.

STEPHEN   I will.

ALEX   We'll juss let 'em come.

STEPHEN   Ennit.

ALEX   Fine.

STEPHEN   Good.

ALEX   Right. Boy screw up his own life, expect me to go
down wid him, he's havin a laugh.

STEPHEN   Will yu stop mumbling?

ALEX   Lasss chance. *(Stephen does move an inch)* Yu goin?
Make up yer mind, Stevie – yu goin or not? Yer mad. Yu are
bloody mad. *(Beat)* What exactly did yu go in a nuthouse for?

Stephen rolls up his sleeves, Alex sees the scars on his wrists.

ALEX   Oh! Yu are stupid, yu got –

STEPHEN *(finishes)* – no brains, yeah!

ALEX   How could yu do summin like that? After all we
went through wid Dad, how could yu?

STEPHEN   I couldn't handle what my life was.

ALEX   And what was yer life – teifing? Yu bin a wort'less
teif all yer life, mate.

STEPHEN   Thass it, thass exactly what I was, wort'less. I look round and I say, 'Stevie – name one good ting yu done in yer whole life', and the answer was nuttin, niche.

ALEX   So yu wake up one mornin, and decide – yeah, I'm gonna kill myself today.

STEPHEN   It was a way out.

ALEX   Yu stupid?

STEPHEN   Well, it was good enuff fer Dad. I'm juss like him.
(Pause)

ALEX   What yu come home for?

STEPHEN   To prove to yu I've changed.

ALEX   Two minute ago, yu were all set to bolt out dat door.

STEPHEN   Awright den, I'll stay. We both will. Whatever yu want. *(goes to touch him)*

ALEX   Move! I don't even know why I'm chattin to yu.

STEPHEN   Don't then.

ALEX   I won't.

STEPHEN   Right.

ALEX   Good. I got half a mind to go myself, yu nuh. Is who yu laugh at? Yu don't think I can – I can.

STEPHEN   Bye then.

ALEX   I can. Cos yer right, yu nuh broth'. What am I holding his hand for? College. He ain't even that bright. I told the fool not to come. And he is a fool. He's the biggest fool there is. Yeah we're fool as well, so what? Ain't his fault he was born last, so what?

STEPHEN   So let's go den. Yu and me.

ALEX   I wouldn't cross the street wid yu.

STEPHEN   Well, then yu ain't going anywhere, Alex. Yu can't. Yu ain't got the guts. Yu best sit yer arse down.

ALEX   Yeah?

STEPHEN   Yeah.

ALEX   Watch me now.

Alex leaves. The front door slams. A few seconds later, Alex comes back into the room.

ALEX *(screams)* Man!

STEPHEN   Yer see?

ALEX   Awright, Mama.

STEPHEN   What?

ALEX   She's still here.

STEPHEN   Yu say I'm mad.

ALEX   Can't yu feel her?

STEPHEN   No.

ALEX *(holds his chest)* In here.

STEPHEN   I said no.

ALEX   Tellin yu what to do.

STEPHEN   No.

ALEX   Yer lying.

STEPHEN   Juss ignore her.

ALEX   I can't, neither can yu.

STEPHEN   Want bet?

ALEX   Yu go then, gwan.

STEPHEN   So was she tellin yu to do then Alex?

ALEX   Yu know.

STEPHEN   Anthoney! – Yer too soft man, yu always do what she say.

ALEX   So go. Go Stevie.

STEPHEN   This ain't fair, Mama, it ain't. Yu want us to watch Anthoney – so what about us, who's watchin us? *(To Alex)* Shut up.

ALEX   I didn't even say nuttin.

STEPHEN   Look pon yu, yu lickle wuss yu.

ALEX   I'm tired, Stevie.

STEPHEN *(copies)* I'm tired, Stevie.

ALEX   Awright.

STEPHEN   Awright.

ALEX	Stop it.
STEPHEN	Stop it.
ALEX	Stephen.
STEPHEN	Stephen.
ALEX	Yu plonker.
STEPHEN	Yu plonker. *(giggles)*
ALEX	It weren't even funny when yu were nine.
STEPHEN	I bet he's tellin them, yu nuh.

ALEX I bet he's shittin bricks. He thinks I hate him. For ben born, for Dad.

STEPHEN	Do yu?
ALEX	Sometimes.

STEPHEN Yu shoulda heard him today, carryin on like sum hard man. 'Ain't happened to me, yet.' Fool man.

ALEX	So what yu gonna do bro'?
STEPHEN	Suppose I better go, den.
ALEX	Yer leavin?
STEPHEN	Yes Alex, I'm leavin. For the police station.
ALEX	Well come, let's go then.

STEPHEN Don't know why yer in such a hurry, they'll think it was me anyway. Even if yu had run and after they pick yu up.

ALEX	Is it?
STEPHEN	Makes sense.
ALEX	Suppose it does. Yer ready?
STEPHEN	I'm ready man.
ALEX	Kid's an idiot.
STEPHEN	Ennit.
ALEX	Yu ready?
STEPHEN	Yes Alex, I'm ready – what yu fussin for?
ALEX	I ain't fussin.

They head for the front door.

ALEX   And what yu mean – when after the police pick me
up? Yu don't think I coulda made it? I coulda made it.
STEPHEN   My arse.

Lights fade.

SCENE 6
*Living room. Stephen comes in. He calls for his brothers. No answer.
He finds his bag. Alex and Anthoney come in shortly afterwards.*

STEPHEN   Yu awright, our kid?
ANTHONEY Hey, less of the kid, man.
ALEX   Oh fer flip's sake Anthoney, he was jokin wid yer.
ANTHONEY Yeah, and I jokin wid him. *(To Stephen)* When did
yu get bail?
STEPHEN   This mornin'.
ANTHONEY They let us go lass night.
ALEX   He knows that.
ANTHONEY I'm juss sayin. Leave me in peace man. Was it me
who ask him to burn the place down?
ALEX   Was it me who asked yu to come?
STEPHEN   Can we not go through this.
ANTHONEY Yeah.
ALEX   Rest up yer lip, 'bout yeah.
STEPHEN   Will yu stop doin that.
ALEX   Doin what?
STEPHEN   Lookin away when I'm lookin at yu.
ALEX   So why yu lookin at me? Ain't me thass lookin
away, it's yu.
STEPHEN   No.
ALEX   Yes.
STEPHEN   So what yu doin lookin at me?
ANTHONEY *(laughs, sees that both of them are staring)* Sorry.
STEPHEN   I'm fine.

ALEX   Come again?

STEPHEN   Thass what yer wondering.

ALEX   I wasn't.

STEPHEN   Yeah, don't strain yerself.

ALEX   Wat yu want me to say?

ANTHONEY *(cutting in)* Seriously?

STEPHEN   Seriously what?

ANTHONEY Yer fine, yu gonna be awright?

STEPHEN   Tell him Alex, tell him if I'm gonna be awright?

ANTHONEY Yu tell me.

STEPHEN   They charged me wid arson kid, done deal.

ANTHONEY And Alex.

STEPHEN   Why yu think they let yu go first?

ANTHONEY Yu takin the blame? Nuh man, that ain't fair.

STEPHEN   I told them it was me as long as they leff yu two
    alone. That was the deal.

ANTHONEY But it ain't fair, though.

STEPHEN   It's done. It was me who did it Anthoney.

ANTHONEY Yer blamin me.

STEPHEN   I didn't say that.

ANTHONEY I can see it in yer face.

STEPHEN   Calm down.

ANTHONEY No.

STEPHEN   I've done time before, Anthoney. I'll be awright.

ANTHONEY No yer not – Alex told me where yu bin.

ALEX *(catches Stephen's look)* What!

STEPHEN   Look, I'll be awright.

ANTHONEY I didn't ask yu to come fer me.

STEPHEN   But we did.

ANTHONEY I didn't ask to be born.

STEPHEN   Stop it. No more blaming yerself, yeah – enuff of
    dat. I'll be awright, man. Ennit Alex?

ALEX   Whatever.

ANTHONEY Do yu have to go court?

ALEX   Yes.

ANTHONEY What yu doing till den? Where yu going? Where yu
stayin? Stay wid us, ennit, Alex? And when yu come out of
prison yu stay wid us then. Ennit? Alex?

ALEX   Whatever.

ANTHONEY Bloody say yes.

ALEX   I juss did.

ANTHONEY Like yu mean it. Give him what he wants, right.

ALEX   Boy love to mek up noise.

ANTHONEY Juss tell him.

STEPHEN   Anthoney shut up

ANTHONEY Thass all we do, ennit? Shut up, we don't say nuttin.
I'm gonna buss yer head Alex if yu don't do it. *(Alex laughs)* I
don't care how big yu are.

ALEX   Boy think him turn man now.

ANTHONEY Juss tell him. What he wants.

STEPHEN   I'm outta here.

ANTHONEY Stephen – wait man.

STEPHEN   Wait fer what? I don't need none a yer.

ANTHONEY Yer lyin, I know yer lyin.

STEPHEN   Laters.

ANTHONEY *(to Alex)* Stephen juss wait, juss wait a minute.

*Alex has plonked himself in Mum's chair. He is reading his paper,
pretending not to care. Anthoney kicks his foot.*

ALEX   Is who yu kickin?

ANTHONEY Will go talk to him.

ALEX   Awright man.

ANTHONEY I said go talk to him, go talk to him.

ALEX   Awright .

ANTHONEY Well, go on then.

ALEX   Awright. Gee! *(to Stephen)* Yu wanna stay wid us?

STEPHEN   Yu askin?

ALEX   Yu wanna stay wid us Stephen – yes or no? I don't care, I don't mind.

STEPHEN   I want my old room back.

ALEX   Whatever.

STEPHEN   Good.

ALEX   Right.

ANTHONEY Hold on a second please... excuse me? Thass my room? *(Alex laughs)* It's my room.

STEPHEN   Juss keep it ready fer me.

ANTHONEY *(gives him the finger)* Keep this!

STEPHEN   Yu carry on like yu got a say in the matter.

ANTHONEY Ca' I do.

STEPHEN   Yu were only borrowin it.

ANTHONEY Yu can piss right off.

STEPHEN   Boy rude man.

ALEX   See what I have to put up wid.

STEPHEN   Him lucky Mum ain't here. Cos she woulda kick up yer lickle backside fer chatting back like that.

ANTHONEY Yeah?

STEPHEN/ALEX Yeah.

ANTHONEY Yeah, so which one a yu is brave enuff to fill in for Mum then? Come now if yer bad. I'll take yu both.

Alex and Stephen look at each other. They smile.

ANTHONEY What? What? Awright yu can juss put yer coats back on.

Alex and Stephen slowly begin to close in on Anthoney who nervously steps back.

ANTHONEY Move. Back off right.

ALEX   What was that move he did again?

ANTHONEY I say back off.

ALEX	Come here for a second.
STEPHEN	Juss fer a second.
ANTHONEY	No. Get off. Get off me. Juss get off.
ALEX	Stephen, hold him, hold him!

Anthoney makes a run for it. Alex and Stephen chase after him.
Blackout.

The end.

Roy Williams

Theatre: *No Boys Cricket Club* (Theatre Royal Stratford East), *Starstruck* (Tricycle), *Lift Off, Clubland, Fall Out* (Royal Court), *Local Boy* (Hamptead), *The Gift* (Birmingham Rep), *Souls* (Theatre Centre), *Sing yer heart out for the lads* (National Theatre), *Night & Day* (Theatre Venture), *Josie's Boys* (Red Ladder).
Television: *Offside, Babyfather* (BBC TV).
Radio: *Homeboys, Tell Tale,* (BBC)
Awards: 31st John Whiting Award, Alfred Fagon Award (1997), EMMA Award for *Starstruck* (1999), The George Devine Award for *Lift Off* (2000), Evening Standard Award for Most Promising Playwright for *Clubland* (2001), BAFTA / Best Schools Drama for *Offside* (2002).

Theatre Centre Productions 1953 – 2003

Most of the following are original Theatre Centre commissions, although we have frequently co-commissioned writers, and produced plays collaboratively, with other theatre companies across the country. Their contribution is gratefully acknowledged.

The Man Born To Be King by Dorothy L Sayers
Sir Thomas Moore
Christopher Columbus by Louis Macneice
Pinnochio adapted by Brian Way
Between The Acts by Brian Way
The Martyrs Of Compiegne by Brian Way
The Magic If by Brian Way
The Storytellers by Brian Way
Grinling Gibbons and the Plague of London by Brian Way
Oliver Twist adapted by Brian Way
Moon Magic by Brian Way
Silas Marner adapted by Brian Way
The Stranger by Brian Way
Midwinter by Brian Way
Leapday Shadows by Brian Way
The Angel Of The Prisons by Brian Way
Meet The Police by Brian Way
The Crossroads by Brian Way
The Signpost by Brian Way
The Wheel by Brian Way
The Ladder by Brian Way
The Bell by Brian Way
The Lantern by Brian Way
The Dog And The Stone by Brian Way
On Trial by Brian Way
The Struggle by Brian Way
The Mirror Man by Brian Way
The Rescue by Brian Way
Mr Grump And The Clown by Brian Way
Valley Of Echoes by Brian Way
The Clown by Brian Way
The Discoverers by Brian Way

The Rainbow Box by Brian Way
The Opposites Machine by Brian Way
The Key by Brian Way
The Survivors by Brian Way
The Island by Brian Way
Balloon Faces by Brian Way
Magical Faces by Brian Way
Adventure Faces by Brian Way
Stream Of Shadows by Brian Way
The World Of Play by Brian Way and Stanley Evernden
Discovery And Survival by Brian Way
Speak The Speech I Pray You... by Brian Way
Nature's Hands by Stanley Evernden
The President by Ronald Chenery
The Sleeping Beauty adapted by Brian Way
Willowit by Stanley Evernden
Puss In Boots adapted by Brian Way
Daring Hands by Stanley Evernden
The Maze by Stanley Evernden
The Valley Of The Sun by Derek Bowskill
The Decision by Brian Way
The Monkey King by Stanley Evernden
In The Game by Derek Bowskill
Gambit by Derek Bowskill
Let's Make A Story by Stanley Evernden
The Season Of Ages by Derek Bowskill
Let's Make Another Story by Stanley Evernden
The Signpost by Brian Way and Margaret Faulkes
Jigsaw / The House by Stanley Evernden
Woman Angel Of... by Derek Bowskill
What A Thing Is Man by Stanley Evernden
Seeking Hands by Stanley Evernden
Timephase by Brian Hayles
Jingo's Journey by David Johnston
Plague '78 by David Holman
Strange Encounters by Chris Denys
Dee's Dream by David Johnston
Witchplay by Mike Maynard
Moving On Up by Chris Denys

Silent Guns by Roger Watkins
Nuts by David Johnston
Bolts by David Holman
Cut! by Mike Maynard
Killed Devised by Coventry Belgrade T.I.E.
Shrewd Woman by Geoff Bullen
Don't Just Sit There by Charles Way
The Stranger by David Johnston
Wild Boy Of Aveyron by David Holman
The Disappeared by David Holman
Kypuru's Cave by Chris Hawes
The Monkey And The Crocodile by Charles Way
Atuk's Return by David Johnston
Imap Inua by David Holman
Wheels by David Johnston
Chairperson by Geoff Bullen
Angels Over Islington by David Holman
Breaking Chains by David Holman
Frankie's Friends by David Holman
Why? by David Holman
Monos Mou Devised
Hollyquinade by Chris Larner
Sir Gawain And The Green Knight by David Holman
Big Cats, Big Coat by David Holman
Drink The Mercury by David Holman
Billy The Kid by David Holman
Red Letter Days by Geoff Bullen
Peacemaker by David Holman
Susumu's Story by David Holman
1983 by David Holman
Bunkers by Jamal Ali
Year One (ABC) by David Holman
Puzzles by David Holman
Inside Out by Lisa Evans
Under Exposure by Lisa Evans
The Zulu Hut Club by Bryony Lavery
Consequences by Lisa Evans
Winners by Yasmin Judd
Face Values by Lisa Evans

Hidden Meanings by Tony Coult
The Mrs Docherties by Nona Shepphard
Over And Out by Bryony Lavery / Music by Helen Glavin
Getting Through by Nona Shepphard / Music by Helen Glavin
Tschioca! Cholova! Devised.
Laughter From The Other Side by Noël Greig
Rip In The World by Colm Ó Clúbháin
Twice Over by Jackie Kay
Stamping Shouting And Singing by Lisa Evans
The Fantastic Forgotten Voyage by Lin Coghlan
Whispers In The Dark by Noël Greig
Pinchdice And Co by Julie Wilkinson
Broken Armour by Noël Greig
When The Bough Breaks Devised.
Sack Of Lies by Julie Wilkinson
The Marx Brothers Go East by Sue Frumin
Familiar Feelings by Noël Greig, Kate Owen and Philip Tyler
A Feeling In My Bones by Lin Coghlan
Just Like A Genie by Jenny Mcleod
Spreading Our Wings adapted by Sandra Yaw
Just My Luck by Adjoa Andoh
Two Marias by Bryony Lavery
A Foreign Correspondence by Tash Fairbanks / Libby Mason / Women's Co.
The House That Jack Built by Mark Holness
Safe As Houses by Thelma Lawson
Listen by Philip Osment
Brave Faces Devised
Feasting On Air by Suzy Gilmour
Chaos by Agnes Limbos
The Secret Garden adapted by Nona Shepphard / Music by Helen Glavin
The Lie Of The Land by Noël Greig
A World Turned Upside Down by Hijinx Theatre
The Visitor by Kate Owen and Max Eastley
The Tower Without Stairs by Jane Buckler
Salt Of The Earth by Diane Samuels
The Snow Queen adapted by Nona Shepphard
The Land Of Whispers by Noël Greig
The Magic Shoes by Nona Shepphard
Dreaming It Up by Noël Greig

Bretevski Street by Lin Coghlan
Mirror Mirror by Janys Chambers
Turncoat by Diane Samuels
Moving Voices by Peter Rumney
How High Is Up? by Brendan Murray
A Fine Example by Angela Turvey
A Spell Of Cold Weather by Charles Way
A Story From The Second World by Anna Furse
Crivelli's Garden by Fiona Graham
Joshua's Egg by Jacqui Shapiro
Under The Bed by Brendan Murray
Common Heaven by Noël Greig
Wise Guys by Philip Osment
Water Wings by Rosy Fordham
Pork Bellies by Molly Fogarty
Positive Mental Attitude by Anthony Gunter
Skin Into Rainbows by Maya Chowdhry
Gorgeous by Anna Furse
Big Baby by Brendan Murray
Souls by Roy Williams
Look At Me by Anna Reynolds
Little Violet And The Angel by Philip Osment
Jumping On My Shadow by Peter Rumney
Breaking China by Fiona Graham
Listen To Your Parents by Benjamin Zephaniah
Devotion by Leo Butler
Missing by Rosy Fordham
Precious by Angela Turvey
Glow by Manjinder Virk
Reality Check (Authentic Voices) by Theatre Centre's Young Apprentices:
Towhida Afsar, Nasima Begum, Dilruba Begum, Rahima Begum, Sophie
Bowman, Shirin Hirsch, Holly Samson, Tunde Sanusi

THEATRE CENTRE
OCTOBER 2003

Founder Patron
Brian Way

50th Birthday Patrons

Bonnie Greer   G. Laurence Harbottle   Diane Louise Jordan
Benjamin Zephaniah

Honorary Advisors
Stuart Bennett   Geoff Bullen   Patrick Boyd Maunsell

Members of the Board of Directors
Irene Macdonald *(Chair)*   Serena Newstead   Saifur Rahman
Sue Robertson   Nettie Scriven   Pat Trueman   Roy Williams

Members of Staff
Jackie Alexis *(General Manager/Deputy Director)*
Alyson Blazey *(Intern)*
Louisa Charles *(Finance Manager (Freelance))*
Rosamunde Hutt *(Director)*
Lesley Jones *(Domestic)*
Michael Judge *(Associate Artist (Education))*
Thomas Kell *(Administrator/Deputy General Manager)*
Iain Lanyon *(Graphic Designer (Freelance))*
Geoffrey Rowe *(Consultant (Freelance))*
Katy Silverton *(Office Co-ordinator/Tour Booker)*
Paul Sullivan *(Press Representative (Freelance))*
Marijke Zwart *(Production Manager/Company Stage Manager)*

Associate Artists
William Elliott   Lawrence Evans   Jane Mackintosh
Paul J. Medford   Bernadette O'Brien

THEATRE CENTRE
Units 7 & 8
Toynbee Workshops
3 Gunthorpe Street
London
E1 7RQ

Tel.: 020 7377 0379
Fax.: 020 7377 1376

admin@theatre-centre.co.uk
www.theatre-centre.co.uk

aurora metro press

Founded in 1989 to publish and promote new writing, the press has specialised in new drama, fiction and work in translation, winning recognition and awards from the industry.

plays for young people

Young Blood, five plays for young performers.
ed. Sally Goldsworthy ISBN 0-9515877-6-5 £10.95

The Classic Fairytales retold for the stage by Charles Way
ISBN0-9542330-0-X £11.50

Three Plays: Jonathan Moore
ISBN 0-9536757-2-6 £10.95

Devotion by Leo Butler
ISBN 0-9542330-4-2 £7.99

Harvest by Manjula Padmanabhan
ISBN 0-9536757-7-7 £6.99

Charles Way: Plays for Young People
ISBN 0-9536757-1-8 £9.95

Best of the Fest. new plays celebrating 10 years of London New Play Festival ed. Phil Setren ISBN 0-9515877-8-1 £12.99

Black and Asian Plays Anthology introduced by Afia Nkrumah
ISBN 0-9536757-4-2 £9.95

Seven plays by women, female voices, fighting lives.
ed. Cheryl Robson ISBN 0-9515877-1-4 £5.95

Graeae Plays 1, new plays redefining disability. ed. Jenny Sealey
ISBN 09536757-6-9 £12.99